LEMON'S HAND BOOK

―OF―

Marshall County

Giving its History, Advantages, Etc.
And Biographical Sketches of Its

Prominent Citizens.

Southern Historical Press, Inc.
Greenville, South Carolina

This volume was reproduced from
a personal copy located in the
Publisher's private library
Greenville, South Carolina

All rights reserved. No part of this publication may be
reproduced, stored in a retieval system, Transmitted in
any form, posted on to the web in any form or by any
means without the prior permission of the publisher.

Please direct ALL correspondence and book orders to:
www.southernhistoricalpress.com
or
Southern Historical Press, Inc.
PO Box 1267
Greenville, SC 29602-1267
southernhistoricalpress@gmail.com

Originally published: Benton, KY 1894
New Material Copyright By:
   Southern Historical Press, Inc.
ISBN #978-1-63914-043-5
All Rights Reserved
Printed in the United States of America

PREFACE.

The object of this little book is two-fold. First, to present to the citizens of Marshall county, in a condensed form, a correct and complete history of the county from its organization down to the present time. Secondly, to collect and compile, in a form adapted to their preservation, important events of an interesting character, together with short sketches and pen-pictures of many of its leading men and women for a period of over fifty years.

In repect to the first object, it may be said that the field has never before been occupied by the historian, and yet we have striven to make it as full and complete as the facts and information before us would justify. This little book, our first attempt, will be closely scanned by the unfeeling critic, but the intention of the writer, and his object in placing it before the public, are, we hope, sufficient guarantees of his good faith to cause his efforts to to meet the approbation of its readers.

The volume then, as a whole, we trust, will vindicate its pretentions, notwithstanding defects which doubtless exist in it, to be considered truly a small monument to the memory of the citizens of Marshall county.

Benton, Ky., December 1, 1894.

MARSHALL COUNTY

The History of Its Organization, Its Resources and Advantages.

MARSHALL COUNTY, named in honor of Chief Justice John Marshall, of the United States Supreme Court, and situated in the Northeastern portion of the Jackson Purchase, is bounded on the North and East by the Tennessee river, which separates it from Livingston, Lyon and Trigg counties; on the South by Calloway county, and on the West by Graves and McCracken counties

Prior to June 1st, 1842, it constituted the Northern part of Calloway county, from which it was separated by an act of the General Assembly of Kentucky, approved February 12, 1842, the first section of which is as follows:

Be it enacted by the General Assembly of the Commonwealth of Kentucky:

That from and after the first day of June, 1842, all that part of Calloway included in the following boundary, viz: Beginning at a section corner, in the Graves and Calloway line, seventeen miles north of the point where the said counties of Graves and Calloway corner in the Tennessee State line; thence east with said section line to the Tennessee river; thence down said river to the McCracken county line; thence south with the McCracken and Graves county lines to the beginning, shall be, and is hereby erected into one separate and distinct county, to be known and called by the name of Marshall; and the seat of Justice thereof shall be established at the most eligible point, as near the center of said county as the faces of the country will admit, in the opinion of the Commissioners hereafter appointed.

Section two provided that the Circuit and County courts of Calloway county should have law and equity jurisdiction till the act became operative. Section three allowed nine justices of the peace to meet on the first Monday in June, 1842, at the house of James Clark, to appoint a clerk. Section eight designated John Wortham, of Graves; Alfred Boyd, of Trigg; Hugh McCracken, of Caldwell; and Charles B. Davidson, of McCracken, to locate the county seat, and allowed them three dollars per day for their services. The justices mentioned in section three, and consisting of James Brien, John T. McElrath, Joseph Staton, Enos Faughn, Joel Gilbert, Robert Elliott, James Stice, Absalom Smith and William Rice met at the house of James Clark, about four miles east of north of the present site of Benton, on June 7, 1842, just on the hill to the right of Spout Spring, and formally organized the first county court. The details of this court were all burned when the county clerk's office was burned, at Benton, on February 29, 1848, and therefore cannot here be given. From the testimony of Henry Hand, first county clerk, taken before a board of commissioners appointed by the court, March 6, 1848, to restore the lost records and consisting of Robert O. Morgan, Joel Gilbert, Francis H. Clayton, Philander Palmer and Thomas McElrath, we learn that the commissioners designated to locate the county seat, "after careful and minute investigation and the examination of circumstances, face of the country, etc.," selected a site for the public square of the county on the southeast quarter of section 32, township 5, range 4 east, being the same upon which Benton now stands. All of the commissioners except Hugh McCracken agreed to this report. The land of the public square belonged to Francis Clayton, after whom Clayton street, in the town of Benton, is now named.

Marshall county has an area of 325 square miles and contains 209,920 acres of land. Its surface is undulating, but the greater portion of it is level. It is well supplied with beautiful streams of living water that enrich the soil and adds to the happiness of man. Clark's river with its three branches, East, West and Middle Forks, is the largest and principle stream that traverses the county. It and its Forks traverse the county from South to North, the bottoms along which these streams run are generally very productive and well adapted to corn and grass, but some of these bottom lands yield very fine tobacco. The West Fork has the best quality of land, which is richly supplied with sand. The Middle Fork is a small stream and has, along its banks, some of the best farms in the county.

Jonathan's Creek is the next largest stream in the county, and it was called "Harland's Creek" until 1818, when its present name was given it. This creek runs across the Southeast corner of the county, is a very beautiful stream and at present has two mills located on it. There are much rich and valuable lands lying in its bottoms, a large portion of which is now in a high state of cultivation.

Bear Creek with its rich bottom lands lies in the Eastern part of the county and empties into Tennessee river a few miles below Birmingham.

Soldier Creek, in the West part of the county, empties into the West fork of Clark's river. Its bottoms are dry and produce an excellent quality of corn, wheat, oats, and a fine quality of tobacco. Grasses and clover of all kinds grow as fine in this bottom as any other part of the state.

Cypress Creek, that runs into Tennessee river, in the northeast part of the county, has high banks in most places, and on each side, almost from its source to its mouth, are as rich farming lands as can be found anywhere in the county. It was thought until a few years ago that people could not enjoy good health along its banks, and, therefore, it would be impossible to clear up and cultivate its lands, with success, but such a theory has been proven false, and now farmers are thickly settled all along its banks and are in the possession of fertile fields that produce abundantly corn, wheat, tobacco, clover and all the grasses.

A short description has been given of the various streams and the rich bottom lands that are to be found along their banks, which constitute at least one-sixth of the farming lands in the county. The hill portion of the county is composed of about five-sixths of its farming lands, and the soil is from four to twelve inches in depth, and is adapted to raising everything that can be produced in the bottoms. Much of the hill lands were abandonded a few years ago, and consequently it was soon covered in persimmon bushes and sedge grass, but since the farmers have learned that such lands can be kept in a high state of cultivation by filling up the gulleys and planting them down in clover and other kindred grasses, they have been fenced in and are now reckoned among the best farming lands on the uplands in the county. These lands are well adapted and are known far and near for the growth of a superior quality of shipping tobacco, which is one of the staple products of the county. Millions of pounds of this article are shipped from here every year.

TIMBER.

The county is well supplied with timber of various kinds, and among the many varieties may be mentioned Hickory, black and sweet gum in abundance, oak in all of its diversified forms, white and yellow poplar of good quality, white ash thoroughly adapted to lumbering purposes, beech, red and slippery elm, sycamore, birch, mulberry, walnut, sugar maple, persimmon, horn bean, ironwood, wild cherry, paw-paw, locust, willow and redbud. Along the streams the growth of timber is luxuriant, affording an abundance of cheap and valuable lumber for all purposes for which such lumber can be used. Within the past few years the timber business has been one of the chief industries of the county and has given employment to thousands of men. There are thousands of acres of fine timbered lands yet in the county that the woodman's ax has never been allowed to invade or destroy.

EARLY SETTLEMENTS.

Much difficulty has been encountered in ascertaining when, where and by whom the first settlements were made. Those who were the actors in rescueing the country from the Indian and the no less powerful enemy of civilized life, the dense forests, had little time, if they had the inclination, to preserve reliable records of their early struggles and hardships. From the old pioneers and citizens of that day and time, nearly all of whom are now gone, and, also, from a paper that was prepared and written by that distinguished citizen of learning and patient research, Philander Palmer, that was read by him at a meeting of the citizens, in the town of Benton, on July 4, 1876, the following facts have been gleaned concerning the early settlements of the county:

Mr. James Stewart made the first permanent settlement on Wade's creek, about one mile north of old Wadesboro, in 1818 or 1819. It is said that the creek received its name from Bannister Wade, who first settled on its banks in the year 1819. It was in this year that emigrants began to arrive in great numbers, so it was then that the following persons settled in what is now Marshall county, (then Calloway.) The following persons settled in township 4, range 3 east: Mr. Daniel, Mr. Bibb, Benjamin and James Knox, Robert and Nehemiah Williams, Arthur H. Davis, James Greer, John Gray, Robert Carney, Stephen Williams, Edward Dillard, Mr. Davis, Samuel Dinwiddie, James Morgan, W. M. Cummins, Mr. Winfrey, Peter Agner, William Baker, Joseph Reaves, Jepthah Griffith, Levi Lamb, John Entrikan, Mr. Thrabe and Henry Darnall. They had settled in the Southwest part of Marshall county, between the years 1818 and 1820. North of them in township 5, range 3, were William Gibson, James Smith, Henry Thompson and John Moore. Still north of them in township 6, range 3, were Stephen and Dr. John Howard. Between the Howards and the Tennessee river there were no inhabitants when the county was sectionized. In the township south of Benton were Murrell Utley, R. E. Rowland, James Bourland, Elijah Goodman who owned an old-time horse-mill, James Jordan, Mr. Twitty, Mr. McDonald, Thomas Goodman, Mr. Benbrook, Mr. Williams, William Riley, Perry Lawrence, Wm. Sneed, Mr. Beech, Mr. Skaggs, James and William Brown, Elijah Veech and James Eaton. In the Benton township there lived Mr. Scott, Moses Clayton, Jesse Thomas and Daniel Ford, Samuel Watson, Mr. Tisdale, Hezekiah Williams, Jesse Jones, John Shumaker, Mr.

Dunn and Mr. Lawson. North of Benton township were Mr. Scott and Mr. Woods, Thomas Hill, Squire Jonathan Hill, Mr. McKinney, Stratton, M. Doon and James Brank. North of this township and on the Tennessee river there were no inhabitants. In the Jonathan Creek country there were Mr. Jones, Bartlet Henson, Isaac Condrum, John Kennedy, John and James Faughn. East of Benton township were James Ashworth, Daniel Nance, Rayden Gray, Wm. Earley, M. Campbell, John Campbell, who were in all probability the men who settled Birmingham, and Joel Yeates and William Short. North of them were Glover Baker, William Whiteside and John Brown. East of them on the Tennessee river were Jeremiah Murray, Wm. Darnold and Benjamin Grindall. Many of these people have migrated and gone to other countries and their family names and stocks have become entirely extinct.

Concerning some of the early settlers and prominent residents of the county, a few interesting facts may be stated:

Isaac Johnston came from Eddyville, Lyon county, some time about 1818–20, and settled near the home of his son, Squire J. H. Johnston, who at present resides at Sharpe. His father, Absalom Johnston, came in the early history from South Carolina, and erected at Sharpe the first horse-mill in Marshall county. Patronized by people for a distance of twenty miles it continued to be, for more than twenty years, an indispensable institution of that section of country. Mr. Johnston was a man of strong constitution and great energy, and it was there he opened up a farm; he was also a member of the Hardside Baptists, and gave great assistance to the work of establishing new churches in the new country. The church grew and prospered until it had 120 members. He finally removed to Smithland, Livingston county, where he died in 1844 or 1845, leaving a family of nine children, including eight sons, all of whom became permanent settlers of Marshall county and leading spirits among the pioneers. Contemporary with those Johnstons were the families of Jack Dooms and James Baker. Where Dooms came from it is not known, and none of his descendants are now here. Baker came from Caldwell county and his sister became the wife of Isaac Johnston and mother of

James H. Johnston. There were two other daughters, both of whom married sons of Absalom Johnston. Isaac Johnston and one brother were soldiers in the Seminole war. Another early family of the Johnston settlement was the Staton's, consisting of Jack, Charles and his son Joseph, who, for many years, was a magistrate. They also came from Caldwell county, and their descendants are now among the substantial citizens of the county. Next came the Briens, Lyles' and others. James Brien came from Logan county, Ky., about 1820, and was one of the first blacksmiths of the county. He was a man of great public spirit and benevolence, just such a one as the pioneer county most needed. He was for several years a justice of the peace, and was sent subsequently to represent his county in the state legislature. He was a member of that body when Marshall county was formed, and earnestly championed the movement. He served in both branches of the legislature. He was a soldier under Gen. Jackson in the war of 1812. He founded the village of Briensburg which still bears his name. He died some years ago, at an advanced age, in less than a mile of Briensburg.

Col. Alfred Johnston was a native of Kentucky, born in Caldwell county, January 22, 1813. At the time of his death, in June, 1873, he was over sixty years of age. When about five years of age, his father moved to Calloway county, then comprehending what is now Marshall county, where he lived till the close of the late war, when he removed to Paducah, the place of his residence at the time of his death. In 1836 he married the daughter of 'Squire Howard, of Calloway county, and reared a family of eight children—three boys and five girls. His eldest son, William Henry Johnston, was slain as a Confederate soldier on the battlefield of Shiloh. His early educational facilities were limited, and yet he was possessed of that large native intellect and inquiring mind, which gave him command of a vast field of information and made him a marked man in whatever position he occupied. The stirring political scenes of his early life, and the partiality of his friends, made him a public officer. He was elected a justice of the peace, the assessor of taxes, then county judge, and then representative to the lower house of the legislature, and, finally, a state senator, all of which positions he filled acceptably. His first contest for the legislature was made in 1844, against Col. Dodd and P. H. Beckham, of Calloway. In 1845 he made his second contest against Col. Dodd alone; and his third, in 1846, against William Wade, esq. In all of these he was successful. In 1849 he made a contest for the senate against Col. James Brien and was elected by 900 majority. This was for the session of the legislature preceeding the revision of the constitution, and this term ended his official life. Withdrawing from politics in 1851 he formed a business partnership with Col. Linn Boyd, at Palma, where he continued till the breaking out of the war. Early in 1861 he enlisted a company in the county and secured its enrollment in the Third Kentucky Regiment, which was attached to the army of Gen. Albert Sidney Johnston, and participated in the battle of Shiloh. By regular promotions he attained the rank of lieutenant-colonel of his regiment, A. P. Thompson being colonel, and served faithfully in the Confederate service for a number of months, when his health failing, he resigned, returned home and took the oath of allegiance to the Federal government.

In January, 1819, William Owen, with Betsy, his wife, and their family, came from East Tennessee and settled on the place now occupied by Alex Smith on Soldier creek. He was probably a Virginian by birth, and was the first white settler in the West half of the county. He and one of his sons were soldiers in the war of 1812, he taking the place of a younger son who was drafted. His daughter, Frances Owen, married Peter Washam, with whom she lived to the time of her death, January 2nd, 1883.

Rev. Henry Darnall, usually known as Harry Darnall, came from Caldwell county in 1819, and settled at the head of Soldier creek, building a small cabin and opening a small farm. He was a Hardshell Baptist preacher, and organized the first church in the Purchase, known as the Soldier Creek church. At first the members met at the house of William Owen, then built a round log house. The organization is still in existence and now occupies a frame building, illustrating not only the doctrine of developement, but that of the perseverance of the saints. He was a man of fair attainments and preached extensively, doing much for the advancement of morality, not only in his own locality, but throughout the Purchase. He died about 1860 at the age of eighty or more, and his wife in 1878, considerably older. He left a large number of descendants, among them, whom, three of his sons Nicholas, William and Henry, became preachers. The first of these was at one time judge of Marshall county.

Robert Rose, born about 1798, in Edgecomb county, N. C., came to Marshall county in 1821. At that time Henry and Benjamin Darnall, William Chambers and Parker Harold were also living in the neighborhood. He often heard of an older resident named Maldin, but never saw him. On Christmas day 1823 he married Polly Darnall, daughter of Rev. Henry Darnall, with whom he lived a period of sixty-six years. This is probably the longest time which any representatives in the county have lived together as husband and wife. They both lived in good and excellent health until a few years ago. From this union have sprung eighty-five grand children, one hundred and ten great grand children, and nine great-great grand children.

Peter Washam came with his father, Peyton Washam, from Hopkins county, Ky., in March 1820, and settled on Panther Creek in the eastern part of Graves county. Father and son came to make improvements on the farm, the wife and mother, Lucy Washam, having remained with the family in Hopkins county. In July she was sent for to visit her husband, who was sick, but became lost in the cane brake on her way, and lay all night near her dying companion, failing to reach him until he was dead. She lived until 1825, and died in Graves county, after which Peter became a resident of Marshall county. Peter used to relate that he, his father and one other man, were compelled to subsist for six days with nothing to eat but a little boiled corn. This was taken, too, from the half bushel of seed corn set aside for the season.

Gen. Arthur H. Davis came to the county about 1821-22. He was a prominent citizen, and represented the Purchase in the legislature. It is said that on December 21, 1821, the state legislature of Kentucky passed an act creating the office of register of lands, and commissioning that officer to offer for sale to the highest bidder in the town of Princeton, each alternate section belonging to the state west of the Tennessee river. The law required the register to offer the land as indicated, and if it failed to bring $1.25 per acre, there was to be no sale. Under this act only one quarter section was sold, Gen. Arthur H. Davis being the purchaser, and the land lying near the town of Benton Marshall county.

John Free, now living with his son-in-law, Calvin Henson, came to the county February 1, 1824. He was a son-in-law of Rev. Henry Darnall. Has always been a good citizen and actively employed in the development of the county.

Daniel Pace, the oldest man in Marshall county, was born February 3, 1792 in Pittsylvania county, Va. In 1806 he accompanied his father to Muhlenburg county, and in November 1825, he came to Calloway county settling a mile and a half north of Wadesboro and entering eighty acres of government land at 50 cents per acre. After paying for his land he had only $5 with which to support himself, wife and five children. In 1828 he entered 160 acres more at 25 cents per acre, and lacked $11 of the amount. This he borrowed of Edmund Curd, the receiver of the land office at Wadesboro. He served in the war of 1812, having enlisted from Muhlenburg county at the call of Gov. Isaac Shelby, who accompanied the troops to Canada. Was participant in the battle of the Thames and saw the dead body of the Indian chief, Tecumseh. The Indian was a man of only ordinary statue. After the engagement his body was badly mutilated, American soldiers scalping him and clipping pieces of skin from his back and thighs. One member of Pace's company brought a piece of said skin home as a relic. For his services during his four months absence, Mr. Pace received at one time $42; then forty acres of land; then 120 acres, and finally a pension of $8 per month since 1871. He held several offices: First that of road commissioner to expend public funds for bridging and building roads. This was about 1828-29. Receiving $1 per day for horse and self, and paid his own expenses. He held also the position of magistrate, and later that of school commissioner. Only one appeal was taken from his decision as magistrate. Mrs. Pace, (nee Lettis Hurt), was born March 16, 1798, in Robinson county, Tenn., and died September 7, 1865, in her sixty-eighth year. She was the mother of twelve children, six of whom are still living. Ten of these twelve children, six boys and four girls, reached the age of maturity and all became members of the Christian church. None ever drank or gambled. Mr. Pace has seen the fruits of his happy marriage, twelve children, one hundred and twenty-three grand children, sixty-one great grand children, and five great great grand children. He joined the Christian church some forty years ago under the preaching of Elder William M. Starks. In politics he served with the Whig party during its existence, and then cast his lot with the Republican party when it was organized. He was a firm friend of the Union during the late war, and, like many of his neighbors, suffered heavily from the depredation of guerrilla bands. He lived until a few years ago, with his son, Hope Pace, about four miles from Wadesboro.

With Daniel Pace settled J. L. Haymes, from Todd county, in 1825. His father was a brother to the mother of Daniel. He served in the Black Hawk war, returning, has, with the exception of two years in Illinois and one in Texas, lived near Mr. Pace's ever since his first location.

Hicks Ray, now living near Harvey, with his son-in-law, Ike Washam, Esq., formerly lived on Duncan's creek, four miles south of the old home of Major Wiley Waller. He came to the county some time during the decade between 1820 and 1830, and has lived the life of a plain, honest christian. He is the oldest man now living in Marshall county, and has been a member of the Methodist church for over an ordinary generation. He is now one of the men who does not believe in the idea that the world is round.

Mrs. Matilda Woodall, who lived and died near Stringtown, about ten miles northwest of Benton, was thought to have been over one hundred years old at the time of her death, which took place only a short time ago. She was among the first inhabitants of the county.

MARSHALL COUNTY'S

GEOLOGIC, ECONOMIC AND AGRICULTURAL FEATURES, ACCORDING TO KENTUCKY GEOLOGICAL SURVEY.

Marshall county has an area of about 324.5 square miles, nearly all of which is uplands, excepting the valley of the Tennessee on the east and north, and the bottom lands of Clark's river, embracing in all about sixty square miles.

The valley of the Tennessee has an average width of two miles on the north between Calvert City and the river, but up the river above Gilbertsville to the Calloway county line, its width is about a mile, greater or less in places. Its surface is uneven, a low and broad elevation of from eight to ten feet high traversing the length of the valley parallel with the river. On either side of this ridge the lands are low and glady. There is but a very narrow strip of bottom land bordering the river. The elevations of Gilbertsville, Birmingham and Aurora are respectively about 339, 347 and 350 feet above the sea.

The numerous streams that enter the valley usually run parallel with the river for some distance, finally cutting across to the latter.

From the valley the uplands rise rather abruptly to from 40 to 60 feet on the north near Calvert City, and 80 feet near Birmingham and Aurora, to the dividing ridge between the waters of the Tennessee and east fork of Clark's rivers. This water-divide is highest on the south, viz: four hundred and seventy-two feet above the sea, and declines northward to 457 at Briensburg, 432 at Scale, 430 at Palma and 417 at Sharpe.

The water-shed of the Tennessee is from five to nine miles in width, and very numerous streams drain the surface of the country, which in the eastern part of the county is very broken and hilly. The divide is very broad on the north, and narrow on the south, presenting altogether a very large area of level and fine farming land.

The drainage basin of Clark's river is but a few miles in width, and the bottom land near Briensburg is one hundred feet lower than that village. During the Paducah overflow, in 1884, back-water from the Tennessee came within a couple of miles of the covered bridge.

The hills on either side of the bottom are quite abrupt, but are probably more so on the north side. The bottom lands are about a mile wide on the north side, but very narrow on the south below Benton, rising six to ten feet to the surface of the belt of level valley lands that on the northwest connect with the broad flats of the Tennessee and Ohio rivers. These valley lands are about a mile in width, very level, and timbered with post oak. South of Benton they merge gradually into the bottoms.

From the flats the country again rises to the divide between the waters of the east and west forks of Clark's river, at an elevation of about 480 feet above the sea, or 125 feet above the river. The surface of this divide is broad and quite level, giving rise to a section of country locally known as the flatwoods. This, as well as the ridge on the north of Clark's river, has a northwest and southeast trend.

The west fork of Clark's river drains but a small section of the county in the southwest corner, its bottom lands being about eighty-five feet below the high uplands.

GEOLOGIC FEATURES.

Marshall county is in the northeastern portion of the old gulf embayment, its eastern border resting on the Subcarboniferous formation. We therefore find in the county a variety of geologic formations, embracing the Subcarboniferous, Cretaceous, Tertiary and Quaternary. The coal measures are entirely absent, the transition from Subcarboniferous to Cretaceous being abrupt.

From the Calloway county line on the south the formations have at first a northerly and then a northwesterly trend, following in their line of outcrop a line parallel with the old shore-line.

SUBCARBONIFEROUS.—On the eastern side of the Tennessee river, in the adjoining counties of Lyon and Trigg, the Siliceous division of this formation rises in high and precipitous bluffs nearly from the water's edge; while in Livingston, on the north, the representative limestone and flinty material are more or less hidden by Quaternary and Subcarboniferous debris for some distance back from the river.

On crossing the Tennessee river into Marshall county, we do not immediately find high Subcarboniferous outcrops, but, after passing the river valley, there is a low shelf or terrace of that formation reaching inland from the river for a few miles, and covered by Quaternary gravel and superficial loam. The limestones have for the most part disappeared, leaving their associated flint layers in place, exposed only in the beds of the streams. On the west the formation suddenly disappears, and, instead, we find the sands and clays of the Cretaceous.

The only points in the county where the Siliceous group appears on high ridges, are on Possum Trot ridge between the forks of Bear creek, and on the sides of the ridges on the west and south of Jonathan creek, near Aurora, in the southeastern corner of the county.

Upon this Subcarboniferous terrace geologists have been unable to find any Cretaceous or Tertiary strata, and the conclusion is plain that it was but a long and narrow belt reaching northward from the Tennessee line through Calloway county, to a point about a mile south of Gilbertsville, or to the edge of the valley, where the river cut its way to westward through the limestones.

In the Tennessee river, one mile below Haddock's ferry, on the Calvert City and Smithland road, there is a long ledge of flint strata extending out from the Livingston county shore in a S. 30 W. course. It rises to about twenty feet above low-water, reaches about two hundred yards from the shore, and has a width of fifty or sixty feet. Its southwest end is only about six feet above low-water, and suddenly terminates. The strata or layers dip eastward very steeply, and at one point are much contorted. It forms what is locally known as the Big Chain.

John G. Lovett.

(For Sketch see page 86.)

A short distance above the ferry there is another line of outcrop of cellular chert in large masses, but without stratification. It is known as the Little Chain, and has a strike across the river of S. 60 W., reaching for 200 or 300 yards from the north shore. The south bank of the river at the ferry shows an outcrop of the cherty masses, and forms an excellent landing. It is covered by 20 feet of micaceous brown loam.

At Barber's landing, just above the mouth of Cypress creek, there is, on the north shore of the river, a high bluff of quartzose sandstone. The bluff is about 40 feet high, overlaid by Quaternary gravel. Its lower layers are thin and much cracked. The rock incloses pyritous spots, and the faces of the layers are much roughened by exposure. In places, the edge of the rock is stained in banded yellow lines, sometimes evenly, sometimes wavy.

Limestone appears one mile southeast of Calvert City in the bed of Cypress creek, and also outcrops on the side of Limestone Hill, one mile south of Gilbertsville. These points mark the northern end of the long Subcarboniferous belt referred to above. Quaternary loam and gravel cover the hills southward to Bear creek, and it is only on the eastern side facing the Tennessee valley that we find the associated sharp flints. No limestone appears here.

The Bear creek hills are high and rough, the main prong of the creek flowing along their eastern base, and in the valley. The ridge between this and Little Bear is known as "Possum Trot ridge." Its summit is 75 feet above the valley, and its sides, almost to the top, are covered with sharp flint fragments of the Siliceous group. The ridge rises southward to the Paducah road, and the Quaternary loam and some gravel covers these Paleozoic rocks.

On the west of the Little Bear the same flint hills are encountered, but disappear to the westward. In the bed of this stream the flint strata appear in regular beds.

One mile southwest of the junction of the two forks of Bear creek there are, on the hills, many lime-sinks, having diameters of from 15 to 25 feet and depths of from 10 to 15 feet, being largely filled by washings from the hill-sides. The ponds that occur north of these are also mostly large sinks that have become filled with water.

South from the lime-sinks, near Mr. Riley's place, on the west side of Little Bear creek, there is, at about 40 feet up on the hill-side, an exposure of hard siliceous rocks, the lower ledge a conglomerate two feet thick, and the upper a bluish quartzite, three feet exposed. They have not been recognized elsewhere in the county.

Going west from Birmingham we find an outcrop of blue limestone forming a ledge in the ridge of the hills that face the Tennessee valley. The exposure continues for one-fourth of a mile southward from the Benton road, and then disappears, the associated flint alone being found on hill-sides to the Calloway county line.

Still further west from Birmingham, the flint fragments are found in the beds of creeks and branches for four or five miles. On the place of Mrs. Lou. Stone, on the head-waters of Buckhorn creek, the flint has decomposed into a whitish siliceous earth, holding some of the flint or hornstone fragments.

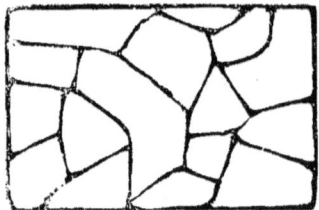

It is brittle or crumbling, and is, in part, stained yellow. It is several feet in thickness. Some of the clay still retains the original form of the flint fragments, as is seen in the annexed horizontal section. The central portion of each block is usually stained yellow.

Southward from Birmingham to Aurora the country is hilly and broken, especially beyond Jonathan creek, between which and the Calloway county line flint fragments are a prominent feature. The hills rise about one hundred feet above the river valley, the flint appearing on their sides to elevations of seventy-five feet above the valley. North-westward, toward Fair Dealing, the siliceous Subcarboniferous group is thus exposed to one mile west of Jonathan creek, while on the Olive and Aurora road its most westerly outcrop is seen on Clear creek, east of Jonathan creek.

CRETACEOUS.—The series of micaceous sands and clays, that have been referred to this formation, form a belt across the county from south-east to north-west, and with a width of from three to six miles. The upper portion of the formation embraces from ten to twenty-five feet of thinly laminated dark micaceous clays, their laminæ separated by thin sheets of highly micaceous and fine white sand. The lower comprises white and yellow sands, laminated and micaceous, with very thin layers of a bluish or light colored, sometimes white, pipe-clay. The layers of clay vary from a fraction of an inch to two or three inches in thickness, and are separated by, sometimes, several feet of sand.

The beds of the formation are covered everywhere by from twenty-five to forty feet of Quaternary gravel and clay, and it is only in bluffs or in banks of creeks and ravines that exposures can be found. Wells, also, frequently penetrate into the strata.

The east fork of Clark's river very nearly marks the western limit of Cretaceous exposures, the upper clays being seen at Dishman's mill, just south of Sharpe on the north-west; again in a well at eight feet in the bottom land four miles south-east of this, and also on the side of the hills opposite Benton.

The latter place shows both upper and lower beds, the locality being known as the "Sand Hill." The hills are from fifty to sixty feet above the bottom lands of the river, and are chiefly composed of loam and gravel, as shown in the following:

1. Brown loam .... 20 feet.
2. Gravel beds in part cemented into a conglomerate .... 10 feet.
3. Light blue plastic micaceous clay .... 2 to 4 feet.
4. Blue micaceous clay in thin laminæ separated by fine micaceous sand and in horizontal layers .... 5 feet.
5. Thin layer of red hematite or iron-stone, irregularly deposited, and in places concretionary or rounded .... 2 inches.
6. Reddish and yellowish micaceous sands, changing to fine white sand at one or two feet—in thin layers, and separated by sheets of stiff, plastic greyish or whitish clays—exposed 26 feet.
7. Sand and clay debris to foot, but probably covering sand strata 15 feet.

The sand bed is in strata with a S. 70 E. dip, as nearly as could be ascertained, and incloses a few concretionary yellow sand nodules which are filled with loose sand.

The upper blue clay bed is again exposed about one-fourth mile eastward up the branch on the road leading to Briensburg. Still further east the Cretaceous beds rest against the Sub-carboniferous rocks

In the northern part of the county, near Little Cypress post-office, on the banks of the creek of the same name, one-fourth mile north of the railroad tank, the Cretaceous clays are exposed in the low bluff, showing the following:

1. Yellow or brown loam... 4 feet.
2. Coarse hornstone gravel... 3 feet.
3. Ferruginous sandstone, uneven... 2 to 4 inches.
4. Micaceous shale or shaly sandstone in thin layers, separated by light slate-colored sand or clay stratum one inch thick. Breaks sharply into fragments... 4 feet.
5. Bluish black clay in very thin laminæ, micaceous and pryitous and separated by very thin sheets of fine white micaceous sand to water's edge... 6 feet.

The sandstone No. 4 splits evenly and thinly, and in places is somewhat quartzose. At another point near this it contains a few rounded and small lumps of black clay.

From the McCracken county line the Cretaceous formation extends north-westward, by way of Paducah, into Illinois.

Going southward from Calvert City, the country is high, and the Cretaceous or other strata are so deeply buried by loam and gravel as to be seldom exposed even in wells. Four and a half miles south, a well dug sixty feet, reached water in white sand. One and a half miles east of Palma, a well passed through six feet of loam, twenty feet of gravel, thirty-five feet of white and red sand, and five feet of sand-rock.

South-east of Benton the Cretaceous belt is narrow, and the clay is buried at sixty to eighty feet below the surface. Three miles south of Olive, the blue micaceous sandy fetid clay was reached at about thirty feet.

On the west side of the river, in the side of the hills, on the road from Olive to Wadesboro, and one mile from the latter village, the Cretaceous clay, light blue and thinly interlaminated with fine micaceous sand, occurs in a ravine by the road-side. This is the most westerly outcrop in the southern part of the county, Tertiary clays being found at Wadesboro.

At Benton, the Cretaceous clays were reached in a well dug at the mill, at a depth of thirty feet, and were not passed through at fifty feet.

TERTIARY.—The Lignitic or Lower Eocene division of the Tertiary formation is alone represented in the county, and underlies all that portion south-west from the east fork of Clark's river, on the line of the Cretaceous.

The *Porter's Creek* (one of the Tennesse subdivisions) beds of blackish clays or "soapstones," alone make up the series, being exposed along some of the streams, occasionally in a ravine that cuts through the superficial gravel and loams, and is also frequently reached in deep wells. The clay is blackish when wet or freshly exposed, and is very brittle under the knife. It is jointed in structure, breaking with a conchoidal fracture, and when exposed to the air crumbles into a grey shale, very tenacious to the tongue.

West from Benton we find the clay outcropping in the bluffs of the middle fork of Clark's river, and again two miles southeast of Stringtown, where a deep pit was once dug into it by parties in search of coal.

The clay is again found three miles south-west of Benton, in wells at a depth of thirty-five feet, and nearer town is seen outcropping in the side of a hill by the road-side.

South from Benton, the "soapstone" or jointed clay is exposed in a branch at Pace's old school-house, two miles north of Wadesboro. The joints are coated with yellowish clay, as at Murray, in Calloway county, and elsewhere.

In Wadesboro, just across the line in Calloway county, the clay is again exposed in a ravine immediately in the rear of the stores. It is deeply ochreous and jointed, and forms a good rough paint

Again, in a well two and three-fourth miles south-west of Nick post-office, the black clay was reached at a slight depth. It again appears along the west fork of Clark's river.

The formation in this county is a part of the belt that passes through Calloway county from Tennessee, and northwestward through this county into McCracken county and into Illinois.

QUATERNARY.—The entire surface of the county is covered by the gravel and loam that belong to this age.

Prior to the gravel deposition, the surface of both the Cretaceous and Tertiary strata had been much denuded, and we find the Quaternary beds at all elevations.

The gravels are the lowest of the series, and, as in other

counties, are made up of more or less rounded fragments of chert and hornstone from the Subcarboniferous rocks, and of all sizes, from an English pea and smaller, to pieces holding fifty or one hundred cubic inches. The usual fossil crinoids, favosites, oolite pieces, occur very generally. The thickness of the beds varies greatly.

In the Tennessee valley no gravel is found. On the Subcarboniferous hills on the west, immediately facing the valley, there is very little; while still westward the bed quickly increases in depth as it recedes from the valley.

The beds are thinest in the north and north-east portion of the county, and vary from five to ten feet. Elsewhere they are from fifteen to twenty feet thick, increasing to twenty-five and thirty as we approach the Calloway county line.

A red sand usually underlies the gravel on the northern and eastern part of the county, and is more or less intermixed with it throughout the entire area.

White pipe-clays are also of no unusual occurrence immediately below the gravel or sand, but are frequently in thin sheets with a fine whitish sand, and inclose pockets of the latter.

The gravel is often cemented into a hard conglomerate by the ferruginous clays and ferric oxide, some of the masses being so firm that a fracture would pass evenly through both the gravel and the cementing material. Such rocks are found especially in the southern and eastern parts of the county, while on the south-east they are in thinner ledges. They are not as prominent a feature of the county as southward in eastern Calloway, and their beds are not as continuous. They often have a thickness of several feet, and are dark red in color, sometimes blackened by exposure or by fire. Small fragments of conglomerate are frequently found elsewhere among the loose gravel as if transported with it.

The rock is sometimes quarried and used for mill-stones, and seem to answer for the purpose very well, but are gotten out and dressed with difficulty. A noted locality is known as Millstone Hill, on the north side of Jonathan creek, and about one and a half miles east of the Fair Dealing and Aurora road. The rock is a conglomerate of white and dark quartz or flint pebbles, and occur in ledges two or three feet thick. It is overlaid by twenty feet of red and hard gravel conglomerate and sand-rock and loose gravel, with some pieces of rounded quartzite, six inches in diameter.

A ledge of ferruginous conglomerate is frequently exposed along the east bluff of the east fork of Clark's river, nearly capping the hills. It is prominent near Benton, and south-eastward near the crossing of the Olive and Wadesboro road. At the latter place it caps a narrow or backbone ridge, seventy feet above the river, and is about four feet thick. It also occurs near New Liberty church on the west side of the river.

The red sand underlying the gravel is often cemented into a hard sand-rock—sometimes massive and sometimes in thin layers. The rock is more generally an indurated sand, which hardens on exposure. It is not usually very firm, and is almost useless as a building material, though sometimes used as underpinning for foundations of small and light buildings.

In the Tennessee valley, the only gravel observed was at Cypress P. O., and thence westward to the county line at Lawton's bluff. It is at a higher elevation than that at Paducah and further down the river, and seems to be the eastern limit of the valley gravel.

The clays that form the lowest of the Quaternary series are of a stiff plastic character, white or bluish-white in color and of various thicknesses.

The most northerly outcrop observed occurs on the place of J. T. Pugh, two miles east of Palma, and at Stice's old mill place, still eastward, near the line of the Subcarboniferous outcrops. At both places some white sand is associated with the clay both in layers and in pockets. Southward the same beds are found at Mr. Frank Burradell's, three miles north-west of Briensburg, and at Scale, where a small pottery was once begun but failed because of want of experienced workmen. Heavy beds are reported as occurring in wells around Harvey, west of Benton.

The brown loam that covers the county, and overlies the gravel everywhere, is in two beds, and has a thickness in this county of from ten to twenty feet. The upper two feet is of a yellowish-brown color, light when drained, and furnishing the best upland soils. Below this it is of a stiffer character, lighter colored, and, as in other counties, is permeated with thin seams of whitish silt.

In the Tennessee valley, the deposit overlying the blue clays is micaceous in character, though otherwise strongly resembling the upland loams.

On hill-sides, the loams are easily washed away by the rains, and huge ravines are of common occurrence. Slides also take place on the sides of steep bluffs, a notable instance of which is to be seen two miles south of Benton, on the east side of Watch creek, and which has resulted in the formation of the "sink" so well known in the county. The hills here are about ninety feet above the creek, and their sides are quite steep. A number of small terraces occur above each other along the foot of the hill, which have clearly been formed by the sliding down of the loams and gravel. The "sink" occurs on the side of the hill about thirty feet above the creek, and is rather rounded on all sides of the interior basin except the west or outside, which is parallel with this part of the hill. The side next the hill is very steep, a continuation downwards of the bluff. The sink has a diameter of about one hundred and fifty feet; the outward sides capped with conglomerate gravel, which prevent them from being washed away. The sink holds water, and has many logs, etc., in it.

Recent Gravel Bed.—In the bottom of Cypress creek, the Paducah and Calvert City road lies for a distance of one-fourth mile along a low elevation of small, loose, but firmly compacted gravel without a loam covering. It resembles the low gravel ridges that cover the loam of the valley at Paducah—a more recent deposit than the loam. It is about ten feet high and fifty yards wide and its trend is N. 60 E.

The Port Hudson group is represented in the valley of the Tennessee by the blue clays and micaceous loams that make up the beds exposed from low-water mark in the banks to the surface of the valley. The clays are in layers of from a few inches to a foot and more in thickness, and interbedded with white, yellow, and red sands. The exposures occur at several points from the Calloway county line on the south, along the river to McCracken county.

The superficial loam accompanies the clay throughout the entire valley. At Birmingham it is fifteen to twenty feet thick. The river here seems at one time to have flowed on either side of the valley, and we are informed that in wells along the river front, and on the west side of the valley, blue clays are reached at fifteen to eighteen feet, while in the central part, comprising a width of about six hundred yards, the clay is not reached at all, but alternating strata of sand and pipe-clay are passed through for sixty feet, water being found between the clay strata.

On the north, at Haydock's ferry, where the valley cuts westward through the Subcarboniferous, the clays do not outcrop on the river bank, the chert and flint rock ledges appearing instead. Toward Calvert City, however the blue and black fetid micaceous clays are reached in wells at ten or fifteen feet.

Again, down the river at Barber's landing, the clays are reached at eighteen feet.

ECONOMIC FEATURES.

The natural resources of the county comprise, chiefly, the lands, timber and pipe-clays, besides small quantities of various other material. All of these have been described in the general report, and it is not necessary, in this place, to give more than a notice of the localities where each occurs, and the general character of the most important.

CLAYS.—The varieties of clay occuring at different points within the county comprise the greyish-black joint clay of the Tertiary formation, and the more recent plastic, lighter colored and more or less refractory pipe-clays, together with a thinly laminated, dark and micaceous, Cretaceous clay, which is exposed in the base of the sand-hill north of Benton, in thin layers, separated by micaceous sand. The latter is again exposed below the foot of the uplands bordering Clark's river bottom near Sharpe.

The black joint clay of the Tertiary occurs to the west of Benton, forming a part of that belt which reaches from Murray, Calloway county, on the south, into McCracken county on the north-west. Exposures may be seen a few miles west of Benton at the foot of the uplands of the middle fork of Clark's river, at Brewers' old mill on the south-west, and near the road three miles south-east of Stringtown, on the north-west. Wherever found, the clay presents the same jointed, massive character, the joints mostly conchoidal in form. The clay is slightly micaceous, black when wet and dark-grey when dry.

The dark color seems to be due to the organic matter which burns out, leaving a grey mass. Chemical analysis shows the presence of nearly forty per cent of sand, one per cent of potash, and a little lime, besides magnesia, iron and soda, and a large amount of alumina. The clay is refractory in nature, but will not take a glaze. It might be used in the manufacture of water jars.

The plastic clays, variegated in color from white to purple, are found chiefly to the east of the black joint variety just mentioned, and always just below the gravel beds.

At Cypress creek railroad tank, in the northern part of the county, there is exposed, in the bed of a railroad cut, made for the purpose of getting gravel for the road-bed, a stiff lead colored plastic clay, finely siliceous and micaceous in character very similar to that found at the Armstrong place, a few miles south, on the east side of Clark's river, in McCracken county. The latter contains nearly two and a half per cent. of potash, and is quite unrefractory, a property that probably also belongs to this Cypress creek bed. The thickness of the bed has not been ascertained, and no tests have been made.

Another lead-colored, micaceous clay occurs in the hill-side at the spring near the house of Mr. J. T. Pugh, a few miles east of Palma. It has a thickness of several feet, is plastic, and fuses with great difficulty before the blow-pipe. At the Rookwood Pottery it formed a white unglazed biscuit, which on glazing became a dark cream color. Its shrinkage on burning was about 15 per cent. This clay contains only a trace of lime, but a little more than one and a half per cent. of potash.

Going southward from this, we find another exposure of the light colored and plastic clay at Mr. F. Burradell's, several miles northeast of Scale. It occurs in some deep washes in the hill-side within an old field east of the residence, and is in beds of from a few inches to about two feet in thickness, separated by yellowish sand, and holding pockets of the same. The lower beds exposed are in thin layers. A specimen from the thickest bed, and as free from sand pockets as possible, was, on analysis, found to contain 70 per cent. of fine sand. After freeing it from the latter, it contained a very little lime and nearly one per cent. of potash. The clay is highly refractory, shrinks about ten per cent. on burning, yielding a milky-white biscuit, which, on glazing, becomes darker.

An unrefractory clay occurs in the bed of a branch on the place of Mr. S. Gray, just south of Scale, and also about a mile west of the latter, where a pottery was once established for a short time. The clay is quite plastic, and with variegated white, bluish and red colors, and occurs in layers from a few inches to as much as two or more feet in thickness, and interbedded with yellow and red sands. A rather broad valley reaches to either side of the branch, and there is, in consequence but little surface covering above the clay. A chemical analysis of a sample of the clay shows the presence of one and a half per cent. of iron, a very little lime, and over two per cent. of alkalies. It is unrefractory, fusing before the blow-pipe, and in the pottery test gave a buff-colored glazed biscuit.

These clays are exposed in other parts of the county, as at Stice's old mill, north of Briensburg, at Mr. Holland's place, a few miles west of Birmingham, and in the hill-sides east of Clark's river on the road to Fair Dealing, but are not of sufficient purity or in quantities sufficient for working purposes. A gypseous variety outcrops in a ravine on the road-side just south of Benton, the gypsum occurring in needle-shaped crystals.

The blue clays, already alluded to as occurring in the valley of the Tennessee river, are well exposed at Highland Landing in the southeast corner of the county. A section at the river bank shows a surface-covering of seven feet of a light brownish micaceous loam, fifteen feet of light bluish clay interlaminated with yellow sands, and ten feet of blue micaceous clay in layers of from one to two feet in thickness; separated by irregular beds of yellow sand with ferruginous concretions. The lower bed of clay is speckled with white and blue particles of the mineral vivianite. This bed is at water's edge. The analysis of a sample of this clay shows the presence of more than seven per cent. of iron, nearly one of lime, and more than three per cent. of alkalies. It fuses before the blow-pipe, and on burning makes a dark red biscuit.

Siliceous Earth or Polishing Powder.—There is in the county a fine floury powder, rather clayey between the fingers, though containing but little real clay, derived from the decay of the chert or flint masses occurring sometimes in the limestone of the Tennessee river section, or in thick masses almost free from limestone. Chemical analysis shows it to be composed of nearly 90 per cent. of silica, from three to ten per cent. of alumina, a bare trace of lime, and from three-tenths to one per cent. of alkalies. No use has been found for this earth, except as a fine polishing material for cutlery. It occurs at several points in the eastern part of the county, especially within a few miles of Birmingham along the base of the hills, and in the region of Aurora. Pieces of the undecomposed chert frequently remain in the clay.

Iron Ore.—Very little iron ore occurs within the county, though some hematite was found on the place of Mr. Cox, four miles west of Birmingham; it outcrops on the side of a hill in his field, in the form of rounded irregular concretionary masses, more or less specular on the inner surface, and in size from small pieces to lumps weighing 15 or 20 pounds. There is, however, no indication of the presence of a sufficient quantity for working.

AGRICULTURAL FEATURES.

Each variety of land, both bottom and upland, that occurs in the Purchase Region, is represented in this county, with the exception of the Mississippi river alluvial and the Bluff or Cane Hills. They embrace the following:

UPLANDS. { Oak and hickory timbered lands.
{ Black-jack and low red oak barrens.
{ Flatwoods.

LOWLANDS. { River valleys.
{ River and creek bottoms

The surface of the country, while rolling and in places hilly, is very generally level enough for tillage, and is all timbered to a greater or less extent. The lands are more generally under cultivation in the central and western parts of the county. The upland crops comprise corn, tobacco and oats, with some wheat the average yields being about 35 bushels of corn, ten of wheat and about 800 pounds of tobacco per acre.

Oak and Hickory or Timbered Uplands.—This designation is popularly applied to those lands having a larger timber growth than what are known as the Barrens or original prairies. They comprise nearly all of the county uplands, and resemble in their features the lands similarly designated in other counties. The surface is much broken and washed into gullies and deep ravines, presenting, on hill-sides, a more or less serrated appearance.

On the divides between the streams the surface is quite level or undulating, affording broad tracts of good farming land. The eastern part of the county is more broken than the western, but the soils of the hills are very similar throughout. The timber growth is red, white and black oaks, hickory and persimmon. The soil is a brownish loam, light and warm where well drained, but where ill-drained is compact, whitish, cold and impervious to water. Decayed vegetation darkens the surface to the depth of an inch or so.

The under-clay, at a depth of about three feet, is also a loam lighter in color, and usually permeated with seams of a light-grey silt, which is almost entirely free from clay. The entire depth to the underlying gravel is from 10 to 20 feet.

The soil is so light and loose that on hill-sides it is readily carried away by rains, the result being the formation of deep gullies. Such are very commonly seen in old fields, and is one of the causes of their abandonment. No analyses have been made of the upland soils of this county, but judging from those made of similar soils of other counties, there is a deficiency of both lime and phosphoric acid, and a fair amount of available potash.

Upland Barrens.—The area embraced in the country known as the Barrens is only about 20 square miles, and lies in the southern portion, being a mere border or offshoot from the large central region of Graves and Calloway counties. The outlines of the region are very irregular, reaching north from Wadesboro about three miles or more, and from the east fork westward to within a couple of miles of the west fork of Clark's river, and beyond the latter to the county line. The streams within this area are usually bordered by a narrow upland belt of larger timber. The soil of the Barrens differs but little from that of the Oak and Hickory Uplands already described, and has a growth of black-jack and red oaks. It is regarded, however, as being especially suited to the cultivation of tobacco.

Flatwoods.—This name is used to designate a broad and level upland region lying a few miles southwest of Benton; and covering an area of about ten square miles. It lies on the uplands that separate the waters of east and west fork of Clark's river.

The surface is undulating, a large portion so level as to be glady, poorly drained, and, in consequence, having a soil that has become whitish, impervious to water, more or less covered or filled with small "black gravel" or bog iron ore, and almost untillable, except by a system of drainage. In those places where there is good natural drainage, the soil is similar to that of other timbered uplands in character and fertility.

The growth of this flatwoods region is post and black oaks, hickory, a little white oak, dogwood and sassafras. On the glades post oak is prominent.

Valley of the Tennessee.—This region, bordered on one side by the Tennessee river and on the other by the high and rather abruptly rising uplands, has a width varying from a mile at the Calloway county line and northward to Gilbertsville, to about two miles on the north of Calvert City, and embraces about 40 square miles. The surface of the valley is uneven, a low river front or bottom lying on the east, and a slough or gum flat occupying considerable space on the bluff side, leaving a low elevation of 15 feet in the center through its entire length, except where cut in two by an occasional stream in its course to the river. The timber of the valley is white and red oaks, hickory and dogwood. The valley is now much under cultivation, especially in that portion from Gilbertsville southward along the central elevation, and toward the mouth of Big Cypress creek on the north. The soils vary from a stiff clayey and crawfishy nature in the flats, to a light micaceous loam on the higher central lands, where natural drainage prevails.

In the broad portion of the valley, north of Calvert City, most of the land is very level and ill-drained, and the soil, in consequence, has a whitish, leached appearance, and is compact and impervious to water. Analyses of these glady lands show the presence of a fair percentage of potash and probably of phosphoric acid, but there is a great deficiency in lime, which, if supplied, would doubtless improve the mechanical texture of the soil, if drainage was attended to, and would also render available much of the large percentage of insoluble potash-minerals present. The glady lands near the mouth of Jonathan creek show a great deficiency of potash and lime in the soil, though the subsoil has a large percentage of the former. The phosphoric acid is present in fair amounts. In the insoluble condition there is a large percentage of potash awaiting the action of lime and weathering.

The better class of valley land, lying at a higher elevation, shows no improvement in composition, its fertility being entirely due to good natural drainage. The soil is said to yield from 50 to 60 bushels of corn, or 15 of wheat, per acre.

Clark's River Valley Land.—The broad flats or valley of Clark's river south of Paducah, in McCracken county, extends up the south side of the east fork into this county. It lies between the river bottom on the one hand and the uplands on the other, in a belt about a mile or less in width, and reaching up the river, with a narrowing width to, and a few miles beyond Benton. Its surface is quite level, and is timbered with chiefly a post oak growth; and its soil is whitish, compact, crawfishy and impervious to water. The absence of any natural drainage makes it cold and unsuited to tillage. Comparatively little undergrowth appears, and the valley is, in consequence, quite open. These lands are probably best adapted to the growth of grain.

Bottom Lands.—The bottom lands of the county comprise but a small proportion of its area, and lie chiefly along Clark's river and the smaller streams. On the Tennessee river there is scarcely any land lower than the valley, the bottoms appearing only here and there and in very narrow strips. On the east fork of Clark's river the bottoms lie chiefly on the north side (the valley flats on the opposite or south side), extending from the McCracken county line nearly to Benton, with a width of about a mile; beyond Benton they continue into Marshall county, and chiefly on the west side. In the region of Wadesboro they widen out because of the junction of several small streams. The bottoms are subject to yearly overflow, and have a good timber growth of red, black, water, post and white oaks, hickory, maple, sugar-tree, lynn, iron-wood, walnut, popular, black and sweet gums, some red gum, elm, catalpa, sycamore, cypress, hornbean, beech and papaw.

The soil is, for the most part, a whitish clay, compact and undrained, and is derived from the washings from the bordering uplands. Because of this heavy nature it is generally untillable, and scarcely under cultivation. The surface portion is darkened by decayed vegetation from the forest growth. An analysis of a sample of the soil from near Benton shows a deficiency in available potash and lime, and a rather fair amount of phosphoric acid. In the insoluble portion there is, however, a large amount of potash which liming would, doubtless, render available.

West fork of Clark's river crosses the corner of the county with a wide bottom well timbered with beech, poplar, gum and oak. The soil is a dark loam, containing more available potash and lime than the specimen from the east fork, though still deficient in these elements. The percentage of insoluble potash is more than one and a half.

The bottom land of Big Cypress creek, in the northern part of the county, is limited to that portion of the creek lying in the uplands, for on emerging into the Tennessee valley the stream cuts its way in a narrow channel westward to the river. The bottom is flat, about two and a half miles in width, and with a length of about six miles from the valley; it receives a number of small and short tributaries. It is largely covered with water, and has a prominent growth of cypress.

The bottom lands of other streams are of no special interest, the soil being more or less crawfishy in character and well timbered.

J. L. HARRIS, Tonsorial Artist.

(For Sketch see page 125.)

District and County Officers.

MEMBERS OF THE STATE SENATE.

In the apportionment for the State Senate in the act of 1840, Marshall or Calloway county was in the 21st district, made up of Calloway and Trigg counties, and was represented by Alfred Boyd, of Trigg, from 1842 to 1846; then by James Brien, from Calloway (now Marshall), from 1846 to 1850. In 1851 Marshall county was placed in the 22d district. Alfred Johnston was senator from 1850 to 1853; Ira Ellis 1853–4; Daniel Matthewson 1855–6 and 1857–8; John L. Irvan 1859–60, called session 1861 and again 1863. The Second Senatorial district was formed by an act of the legislature 1860 and was composed of Ballard, McCracken and Marshall. The following Senators have served since 1863: W. T. Chiles from December 7, 1863, to January 4, 1865, when J. M. Bigger took his place until 1866, after which Oscar Turner served 1866–70; J. C. Gilbert 1870–74; Samuel H. Jenkins 1874–78; G. W. Reeves 1878–82; John W. Ogilvie 1882–6; T. L. Glenn 1886–90; John W. Ogilvie 1890–94.

MEMBERS OF THE HOUSE OF REPRESENTATIVES.

The following are the names of the men who have represented the county since 1851, when the old constitution went into effect: Robert O. Morgan served in 1851–3; James Brien 1853–5 and 1865–7; Wiley Waller 1855–7 and 1863–5; Thomas L. Goheen, Sr., 1859–61; Jesse C. Gilbert 1861–3, and was expelled (because connected with the Confederate army) December 21, 1861, and was succeeded by Wiley Waller 1862–3; Basil Holland 1867–9; Lacy Hibbs and C. H. Webb from Livingston and Marshall; W. J. Stone 1875–83 from Marshall and Lyon; J. W. Dycus 1879–80; W. M. Reed 1877–8 and 1885–6; W. C. Holland

1887-8; J. J. Nall 1889-90; J. C. Glenn 1891-2-3; J. W. Graham 1894-5. Alfred Johnston served during the years 1845-6-7 from Calloway and Marshall counties.

Dr. Samuel Graham, of Briensburg, was a member of the Constitutional Convention from Marshall and Lyon 1890-91, and he was reckoned among the wise, safe and patriotic members of that convention.

CIRCUIT CLERKS.

Old citizens assert that the first clerk was Irvin Anderson. The records, however, commence with Henry Hand, the efficient county clerk, who held till the new constitution came into operation. R. F. Stone held from June 11, 1851, to December 23, 1853, when he resigned, and was succeeded by S. H. Starks, who was appointed to discharge its duties, which he did till his death in 1855. Moses Riley, appointed successor, held the place till 1861. J. H. Riley, his son, discharged the duties of the office from June, 1862, till June, 1863, and again from July, 1865, to February, 1867. W. D. Hunter held from June, 1863, to December, 1864. He was followed by G. S. Jones from December, 1864, to July, 1865. C. C. Coulter, who died a few years ago at Mayfield, held from February, 1867, till he resigned in June, 1871, when J. O. Johnston qualified and held till December, 1880. At this time T. F. Palmer, son of Philander Palmer, the first attorney of the county, was elected and discharged the duties of the office for a full term of six years, after which he moved to Mayfield, where he died a few years afterward. He was succeeded by his youngest brother, Solon L. Palmer, who performed the duties of that office with marked ability for six years. When his time as circuit clerk expired he was made cashier of the Bank of Benton, which position he now holds. He was succeeded by Robert L. Shemwell, who was born and raised near Oak Level, and is now discharging the duties of that office in a manner entirely satisfactory to his constituents.

COUNTY JUDGES.

Under the old constitution the duties of this office were performed by magistrates. The office began with the adoption of the new constitution in 1851. The first officer was James Stice, who was elected in June, 1851, and served till his death in 1852. Following him was Alfred Johnston, who served about one month. He was succeeded by T. L. Goheen, Sr., who continued from September, 1852, till September, 1858; J. M. Stephens 1858 to 1866; W. A. Holland 1866 to 1870; J. W. Dycus 1870 to 1874. In September, 1874, Rev. Nicholas Darnall, son of Phillip Darnall, was qualified and held the position till March 4, 1878, when he resigned. In the canvass he promised to serve the people for $300 per year. This fact, combined with sympathy, resulted in his election. T. L. Goheen, Jr., county clerk, was de facto judge during the early part of the term, and W. B. Ely, J. P., during the latter part. T. L. Goheen, Sr., was appointed by the magistrates March 4, 1878, and continued till the following September, when W. P. Lee came into office. He was re-elected at the end of his first term and made the people of the county an excellent Judge during the eight years which he served them. He was considered one of the most attentive officials the county ever had. He is now a citizen of Mayfield and was elected county judge of Graves county at the recent November election. In August 1886 Elias Barry was elected county judge and served the people acceptably for four years. He was succeeded by John J. Dupriest, who was elected as an independent democrat in August 1890, and served the county as a faithful county official until his term expired under the new constitution January 1, 1895.

COUNTY ATTORNEYS.

Pleasant H. Beckham was sworn in at the organization of the county in June, 1842. On December 4, 1848, the court appointed Philander Palmer, and annually, thereafter, till June, 1851, when under the new constitution, he presented a commission from Governor Helm as the regularly elected officer. He held this office till April, 5, 1856, when he resigned. Philander

Palmer, was born in New Hampshire, December 8, 1817; graduated from Norwich University, Vermont, and then came to the upper counties of Kentucky, where he read law with Judge Pryor afterwards, and at present a member of the supreme court of the state. Having taught school he came to Benton about 1844, with all his earthly possessions tied up in a small valise. He opened the first law office in Benton and became the Gamaliel of the county. In 1849 or 1850 he married Susan A Whittemore, with whom he lived till the date of his death, March 6, 1880. He was the leading spirit of Marshall county and gave his best energies to its development. R. F. Stone was appointed April 7, 1856, to fill out Palmer's term and again October 1857. The records next show J. C. Gilbert as appointed October 1865, followed by Henry Dodd, who held till 1870, when W. A. Holland was enstalled. In 1874, he was succeeded by J. W. Dycus, who resigned in 1875, when W. M. Reed was appointed. He continued till November, 1879, when he resigned and was succeeded by Ed Palmer, son of Philander Palmer, who served till 1882. He was succeeded by J. M. Fisher, who served for two full terms of four years each, making the county an able and efficient county attorney. His term of service ended the first Monday in September 1890, when he was succeeded by H. M. Heath, the present efficient county attorney, whose term will expire January the first 1895.

COUNTY COURT CLERKS.

Henry Hand held this important place from June, 1842, the date of organization, through the remaining period of the old constitution, and under the new, up to August, 1853, when he resigned and was succeeded by Jesse C. Gilbert, who held the office till September, 1858. At this time John W. Dycus came into power and held it till September, 1870. September 5, 1870 T. L. Goheen, Jr., was sworn into office and held it till October 24, 1880. He was suddenly stricken down by an overdose of chloroform, taken for medical purposes. He stood six feet, seven inches in height, and was a popular man in the county.

He died at the age of 36, a member of the Knights of Honor and Free Masons, and his picture may be seen at Lemon's drug store. J. L. Childs was appointed to discharge the duties of the office until the ensuing August election. At this election W. J. Wilson was chosen by the voters of the county. He qualified as county clerk on August 6, 1881, with T. E. Barnes and E. Barry as sureties, who have acted as his bondsmen continuously from that day until his present term of office will expire, which will be on January 1, 1895. He is an obliging popular county clerk.

COUNTY SHERIFFS.

Thomas Ford, Enos Faughn, Peter W. Gardner, Joel Gilbert, Henry B. Williams, Moses Riley, Samuel Duncan and Phillip Darnall occupied this responsible position in regular succession from June 7, 1842, to January 1861. During the period of the war it was filled more or less irregularly by William N. Peterson who resigned and went into the Confederate service; Philander Palmer, A. A. Nelson, jailer, who acted as sheriff, James Story assisting; W. B. Ely and G. S. Jones. Subsequently it was held by H. M. Wade, T. M. Freeman, M. C. Rowland, A. A. Nelson, W. W. English, C. H. Starks, J. H. Little and C. H. Starks was again elected and is the present encumbent.

COUNTY JAILERS.

John J. Averitt, Robert Clark, R. O. Morgan, C. E. Miller, N. B. Roach, A. A. Nelson, H. Johnston, Henry L. Minter, Thomas E. Barnes, J. R. Troutt, John M. Stilley, J. Q. Thompson, J. F. Brandon, J. T. Ozment, Jesse Lindsey and Pete Ely, have in succession held this important trust. Mr. Nelson served twice, once during the opening of the war, and again from 1870 to 1874. Pete Ely is our present efficient jailer, and his present term will expire January 1, 1895.

SCHOOL COMMISSIONERS.

At first there were three, then six, and afterwards but one commissioner. The successive incumbents were Hugh Gilbert, Sr., Daniel Pace, William H. Stone, J. M. Quarles, Rev. D. M. Green, J. T. Stone, Joshua Barnhart, John Gilbert, J. O. Johnston, W. A. Holland, Elias Barry, Louis Fields, J. M. Fisher and C. H. Starks. In 1884 the name was changed from commissioner to superintendent and M. B. Pace was the first to fill the place under the change. He was succeeded by Louis E. Wallace who performed the duties for one term of four years, succeeding himself for another full term and is now performing the duties of the office to the satisfaction of the people.

COUNTY ASSESSORS.

Hugh Gilbert, J. C. Miller, Hugh Arant, T. T. Grubbs, D. D. Thompson, W. M. Jones, J. H. Flower, J. M. Helm, W. B. Jones, A. J. Starks, T. L. Goheen, J. A. Clark, J. B. Fletcher and J. M. Johnson, the present officer who is serving the people a second term in this capacity, constitute the number of assessors of the county from its organization to the present day.

COUNTY SURVEYORS.

Marques Barnett, L. T. Barnett, his son and deputy, A. W. Thomas, J. G. Haydock, Thomas F. Harrison, O. T. Williams, Hamilton Perry and Ben F. Sears constitute the names of the surveyors of the county from its organization to the present time.

TRUSTEE OF JURY FUND.

This trust has been held by Henry Hand, R. F. Stone, S. H. Starks, Moses Riley, J. W. Dycus, C. C. Coulter, J. O. Johnston, N. R. Reed and W. J. Wilson, the present trustee.

The County's Soldiers.

The county was very young when the Mexican war broke out, and of course there were but few people living in it, yet she furnished her part of volunteers for the army. There was quite a number of our best young men went and joined the army and made brave and gallant soldiers, but they have nearly all fought life's last battle and have gone to join the silent army of the dead. At present we know of but five Mexican soldiers living in the county: Wm. Reeves, Wat Austin, Charles Littlejohn, Elnathan Elliott, and Milton Bowerman.

For the Confederate service two companies were organized, the first by Alfred Johnston, and the second by Crittenden Edwards. These two companies were attached to the Third Kentucky Infantry and served with Gen. Albert Sidney Johnston's army in the battle of Shiloh, near the Tennessee river, where it suffered severely. These companies continued through the war. In these companies were the following officers by appointment or promotion: Reason Ratcliffe, captain; R. F. Stone, of Benton, captain, and killed at Shiloh. He was succeeded by Felix Staton as captain. John Morgan, who resides near Benton, became first liutenant, and made a brave and gallant soldier. Williams Owens, who now resides in Graves county, was second lieutenant, and Harrison Hall, recently of Oak Level, but now of Benton, third lieutenant. Other citizens of the county enlisted in other companies in Confederate service from other counties.

In 1861, from the state militia and other sources, a company of men was organized for the Union army by Col. Thomas B. Waller, now living in Mayfield, Ky. This company was attached to the Twentieh Kentucky Infantry. At the organization he became captain of the company and was finally promoted to be major, and later on lieutenant-colonel. This regiment had some experience that it did not enjoy. It was captured by Gen. John H. Morgan at Lebanon, Ky., in July, 1863, and its prisoners compelled to run to Springfield, a distance of eleven miles, where they were all parolled. Benjamin Rush Waller was a lieutenant in the same regiment. Maj. Wiley Waller, who died a few years ago, near Harvey, Marshall county, organized the first Battalion, Sixth Kentucky Calvery of company C. with J. H. Starks captain, composed of men from Marshall, Calloway and McCracken counties, and company D. with Thomas Carter captain, composed of men from the same counties, and a lot of refugees from Tennessee. Attached to it was a battalion of the Fifteenth Kentucky Calvery, consisting of five companies under the command of Lieut-Col. Henry, of Princeton, Kentucky. He being attached to command Fort Heiman, on the Tennessee river; the battalion was assigned to Maj. Waller. It consisted of company A. recruited from Marshall county by Captain Samuel Duncan of Benton; company B., Captain Samuel Purcell of Graves county, formed mainly from McCracken and Graves; company C., Captain Belt, formed in Livingston and Caldwell; company D., Captain Maxwell, of Princeton; company E., Capt. Lewis A. Hanson, Graves county. This command was organized at Paducah and served from October, 1862, to October, 1863. After the expiration of twelve month's service many of them re-enlisted under Maj. George F. Barnes, a brother of T. E. Barnes, of Benton, in the Sixteenth Kentucky, the history we will not here give.

Marshall county suffered some by the war, but not so much as other counties in the state. Horse stealing was about the worst trouble with which our people had to contend, until just before the close of hostilities several marauding bands of lawless men made life a little unpleasant for our citizens.

We are not in possession of the number of men who enlisted in either the Confederate or Federal armies from this county, but there was quite a large number who fought gallantly for the cause of the south, and many went from here that have never returned, but whose bones now lie bleaching on various battle fields of the south. Probably a like number saw fit to give their lives for the cause of the Union and for the upholding of the stars and stripes and the overthrow and destruction of the Rebellion, many of whom returned and are here and elsewhere following their choice avocations as true, loyal American citizens, while many perished on the battle fields, and others have followed since the close of the war.

The United States government has been kind and generous to the Federal soldiers and has passed many laws favorable to them in the way of paying them pensions. There are a large number of old soldiers that were wounded or became disabled on account of sickness brought on by exposure during their services in the army that are now drawing liberal pensions from the Federal government who still reside in this county. Many poor widows and orphan children are made happy, and the wolf kept from their doors on account of the pensions they draw, because of a dead husband or father that gave his life and spilled his blood upon the altar of his country for what he conceived to be right and patriotic. But a period of thirty years has thinned them out, and in less than thirty years more hardly one will be left in this county to detail the terrible horrors of war.

The First Hanging.

The first man that was ever hung, until he was dead, for taking the life of his fellow man in this county was Achilles Peay, a slave who was then the property of William Peay. He was hung on June 16, 1854, near where Mrs. Etheridge now lives in the southeast part of the town. He was hung for stabbing Jake Palmer, a slave belonging to Philander Palmer; the difficulty took place in an old cabin situated on the lot now occupied by the residence of W. A. Holland. The wounded man lived for four or five days before he died; he died on the hill just west of where Mr. Parker now lives. It was a public hanging and took place in the presence of a large crowd of people.

The Second Hanging.

Soon after the war, when the minds of the people were more or less disturbed, Samuel Gaines was arrested for the murder of B. F. McNabb. The killing took place near the home of Mr. McNabb, in the southeast part of the county, while he was out in his clearing. He was shot down in March, 1865, by Samuel Gaines and McDonald Hamilton. They were both indicted at the June term of the circuit court of the same year, and the indictments were returned on the 28th day of the month signed by John B. Dupriest, foreman. The case was called at the same term of court the indictment was found, when both parties announced "ready." Chas. S. Marshall was on the bench with W. W. Tice, commonwealth's attorney, assisted in the prosecution by Col. Ed. Crossland. The defendants were represented by P. Palmer and J. C. Gilbert. G. S. Jones was sheriff, assisted by his deputy, John J. Dupriest, our present county judge. James H. Riley was the clerk and Henry L. Minter the jailer. The jury that tried the case are named as follows: C. Mathis, Wm. Dunn, C. B. Bond, Elijah Johnson, Sam Dees, Joe Alford, W. H. Copeland, Eli Wallace, John Minter, Jesse Reeder, John Edward and David Shemwell. The verdict was as follows: "We, the jurors, do find the defendant guilty as charged in the indictment.—David Shemwell, foreman." Judge Marshall set September 15, 1865, as the day upon which the prisoner should be hung, but his friends liberated him from jail and he and Hamilton both made their escape, but the next year they were both caught and brought back. Gaines was caught near Louisville by a Mr. Tice, a Methodist minister from Calloway county, for which he received a reward of $250. Governor Bramlet commuted the death sentence of Hamilton to ten years in the penitentiary, which time he served out and spent the remainder of his days in Tennessee, but the governor fixed July 13, 1866, as the day for the execution of Gaines. The scaffold was erected in what is now F. M. Pool's field, just below where his residence now stands, and on the day fixed Samuel Gaines paid the penalty of his crime in the presence of an immense gathering of people.

The County Courthouse.

The first courthouse was built of logs and was erected by Francis Clayton about 1843, but in 1847 it was found to be insufficient for the business of the county and it was sold to the man who built it in 1848 for $26. It was located near the southeast corner of the public square.

The second temple of justice was erected in 1847, at a cost of $6,000, exactly on the spot where the new one now stands. The principal contractor was Thomas McElrath, but the wood work was done by Lewis Henderson, who lived and died near Olive, this county.

The present beautiful courthouse was built in 1888, on the ground where the old one stood. M. Lewman & Co., of New Albany, Ind., were the contractors, and John McKinnon, the architect. The legislature passed an act authorizing the county court of claims to build a new courthouse, and for that purpose the court appropriated $14,000, all of which was used in building and furnishing the present imposing edifice. The people of the county, at first, were very much dissatisfied with the appropriation, but since the house was built they are glad of it and are well pleased with it.

The County Clerk's Office.

The first clerk's office was a wooden structure, and was built on the public square in front of where Barry & Stephens' business house now stands. In 1848 it was sold for $9.12½, but in 1860 another office was built near the center of the square at a cost of $1,500. It was torn down in 1888, when the county clerk's office was located in the northeast corner of the new courthouse, where it is at present located.

The County Jail.

The first jail that was built in the county was a log structure, and it was erected by John Hiett and Dillon Ford, about the year 1843.

The second one was built in 1853-4, at a cost of $1,600. It was built of brick, and the contractor was Nathan Bowman, of Calloway county, with Thomas McElrath as his surety. Though it was built on the old style, yet it was a safe and substantial building. With the increase in population came the increase of crime, and it was in the year 1883 that the county court of claims ordered the old one torn down, and upon the same lot a new one erected.

The new and present county jail was built by Cosby & Landrum, contractors, of Mayfield, Kentucky, at a cost of $5,224. D. A. McKinnon, of Paducah, Kentucky, was the architect. The new jail was not a safe one, and was badly constructed, and since it was built several prisoners have made their escape from it, but recently it has been repaired in such a way as to make it one of the safest and best jails in this part of the state.

No Home for the Poor.

The county has never yet seen proper to build and own a poor house. The poor are let out at public outcry, each year, to the man who will keep and feed them at the least expense to the tax-payers of the county. This is said to be the cheapest and best way to care for the poor, and, consequently, no poor house has ever yet been erected by the county.

Churches of the County.

When the early settlements began in the county there were no church houses, but as long as men and women have lived in the county so long has there been christians and workers for the Master's cause. No people, it matters not where they lived, had a higher appreciation for the doctrines of the Bible than the people of this county.

Among the early settlers of the south and west part of the county were to be found such zealous ministers in the Baptist church as Henry Darnall, Absalom Copeland, James Bell, Hugh and Ambrose Gilbert. It was then, as it is now, the "old time" Methodist circuit riders were, at least once in each month, to be found at all convenient and accessible points preaching to the people the unresearchable riches of Christ. They were the first to preach at stated intervals to the people, and for over seventy years they have been proclaiming the doctrines of their church.

Morgan Williams was the pioneer preacher at Wadesboro and vicinity, while Dr. John Johnson preached to the people further north in the county. Calvin Philley represented and preached for the Presbyterians in the north part of the county and did good work for his denomination. It was not long after this portion of the state was settled up before the ministers of the Christian church made their appearance. Among the first ministers of that faith and order to preach the apostolic doctrines of the Bible were Elders Marshall Starks, James Lindsey, Sr., J. F. Mecoy and James R. Jones. At the time when these soldiers of the Cross began to proclaim and preach their peculiar views of the Bible, as taught by Alexander Campbell, the Christian church was very unpopular and met with much bitter opposition, from all the other churches, but a half century has wrought a wonderful change in public sentiment, and now the

Christian church is one of the most popular and influential religious denominations in the county.

The Primitive Baptists, the Missionary Baptists, the Methodist Episcopal Church South, the Cumberland Presbyterians and the Christian church, all have strong followings in the county. There are no Catholic or Episcopalian churches in the county; there are however, a few churches of the Methodist Episcopal Church, or as they are sometimes called Northern Methodists.

THE NAMES OF THE CHURCHES.

For the information of the people who may now or hereafter read this book, the names of the churches, the time when organized, the present number of communicants and the names of the pastors as near as could be ascertained, is hereby given

CUMBERLAND PRESBYTERIAN CHURCHES.

Of this denomination there are only four organized churches in the county.

OAKLAND CHURCH was organized in the year 1859 by Rev. T. S. W. Russell with W. B. Walters, James Leckey and Ewing Dishman as its ruling elders. T. S. W. Russell served as the first pastor for four years; then the Rev. J. D. Kirkpatrick was called to the pastoral care of the church, which position he has held on down to the present time, with the following exceptions, the Rev. Wm. Ward, one year; C. G. Kennedy, two years, and J. E. Edwards, two years. The church conducts a live Sunday School, a Young People's Society of Christian Endeavor, and a Woman's Missionary Society. The church is located in the northern part of the county on the Benton and Paducah gravel road, and has a membership of 115.

THE PALMA CHURCH was organized in 1867 by the Rev. J. D. Kirkpatrick, who has been its pastor from that day until the present, except that Wm. Elliott served one year, J. V. King two years, and J. E. Edwards two years. The church conducts a Union Sunday School with the Methodist Church South in the same house. The Rev. J. D. Kirkpatrick is the present pastor and the church has a membership of 40.

THE BIRMINGHAM CHURCH was organized a few years ago and much of the time since its organization it has been without a pastor, and therefore it has not been much of a success. It conducts a Union Sunday School in connection with the M. E. Church South. It has a membership of 20 and the Rev. J. D. Kirkpatrick is its present pastor.

UNITY CHURCH is located in the southeast part of the county; its membership is not known, but the Rev. J. V. King is its present pastor and has been for years.

There never were many preachers of this denomination in the county, the ones, however, that have labored most zealously for the upbuilding of the church were such men as J. D. Kirkpatrick, J. V. King and Charlie G. Kennedy, all of whom are yet living. J. D. Kirkpatrick was born in Montgomery county, Tenn., November 27, 1828, came to and located in McCracken county, Ky., in January 1848, but in 1866 he came to Marshall county near where he now lives, in the northwest part of the county, near the McCracken county line. He was married in April, 1850, to Miss M. J. Rudolph. He began preaching in 1855, but was ordained to the whole ministry in the fall of 1856 since which he has given most of his time to preaching for the salvation of sinners.

This denomination has a membership in the county of about 225.

PRIMITIVE BAPTIST CHURCHES.

There are six Regular or Primitive Baptist churches in this county, as follows: Soldier Creek, New Hope, Union, Middle Fork, Rough Creek and Mount Moriah.

SOLDIER CREEK, which was originally Clark's River, was constituted on Saturday, May 13, 1830, with 12 members, by Elders Wolf and Payne as a presbytery, and being the first church constituted in Kentucky west of Tennessee river, the legislature gave said church eight acres of land, which it still owns, and on which is one of the oldest as well as one of the largest burial grounds in the county. The membership of Soldier Creek at present number 59. Elder J. P. Jenkins is the present pastor. The monthly meetings are on the Second Sunday in each month, with the Saturday before.

NEW HOPE may justly be called one of the pioneer churches of this county, but we have not the date of its constitution nor of the presbytery who constituted it but it is safe to say that it has had an existence for more than 50 years. It has a very comfortable house of worship, three acres of land for church site and burial ground. T. R. Bolton, the clerk and one of the deacons, is one of the earliest communicants, and is still living at the advanced age of 85 years. Present number of members 32. Elder J. P. Jenkins is the pastor.

THE CHURCH AT UNION was constituted about the year 1842 but by whom and how many members in the constitution we have failed to learn. It has had an existence for about fifty-two years. It has a reasonably comfortable house of worship. Present membership 51. Elder T. F. Harrison, of Oak Level, is and has been the pastor for 10 or 11 years past.

THE CHURCH AT ROUGH CREEK, for many years under pastoral care of Elder James Henson, deceased, finally went down and became extinct as a church, but on June 26, 1880, it was re-constituted by Elders T. W. Hutchens and W. D. Poyner, with six members. Present number of members, in October, 1894, twenty. Monthly meeting, the Fourth Sunday and Saturday before in each month.

THE CHURCH AT MT. MORIAH was constituted in May, 1870, with 12 members, by Elders G. Gibson and E. Watkins and Deacons T. R. Bolton and W. G. Atwood as a presbytery. Present membership, (Sept. 1894), numbers 71. Elder Thos. F. Harrison, of Oak Level, has been chosen for the pastor each year for 18 or 19 years. The monthly meeting are on the 2nd Sunday in each month and Saturday before.

MIDDLE FORK CHURCH was organized on Friday before the Fourth Lord's day in December, 1842, at the house of A. McManus, three miles west of Benton. The presbytery was composed of Elders Harry Darnall, H. Gilbert, Wm McGrigor and F. Norman J. McBride. F. Clayton was chosen spokesman and the following letters of dismission were then given in: N. Copeland, Briant Roach, F. H. Clayton, James Laremer, Sally Copeland, Penelope Laremer, Martha Laremer, Nancy Roach and Thos Morgan. This church was organized on the principles of

L. E. WALLACE, COUNTY SUPERINTENDENT.
(For Sketch see page 88.)

the Soldier Creek association. F. H. Clayton was elected clerk, and he was also appointed to prepare abstracts of principles and rules of decorum. H. Darnall was chosen moderator, F. H. Clayton, deacon. The agreement was then made to hold their monthly meetings on Saturday before the fourth Lord's day in each month, which has continued to be their day of worship ever since. At the April meeting, 1843, Elder Hugh Gilbert was chosen pastor, and continued until March, 1844. Elder Wm. McGrigor was chosen pastor in June, 1844, and continued as such until April, 1845. At the same meeting Eld. Granville Gibson was chosen the pastor and continued until November, 1883, when Elder T. F. Harrison was made pastor, and has been continued as such until the present time. W. C. McGrigor was chosen clerk of this church at the June meeting in 1860, and has continued to hold the same position until the present time. The church when organized, in 1842, had nine members, and 30 members in 1894.

METHODIST CHURCHES.

The first Methodist church that was organized in Jackson's Purchase was organized in what is now Marshall county. The church was organized by Parson Ogden, in the year 1823, at the home of Farrar Dunn, about midway between Benton and Birmingham, and was called the Dunn church for three years, when the name of Mt. Vernon was given it. The first church house was built in 1826; Farrar Dunn and wife, Carson and wife McGilberry Wyatt and wife, Hiram Bourland and wife, Elijah Collie and wife, Smith Brown and wife, Wiley Harp and wife, and Newton Johnson and wife were among its charter members. In 1823 it had 18 members, and in 1840 its membership was 152. Mount Vernon church continued under that name until 1852, when its name was changed to the Briensburg and Arkadelphia churches. Joseph Dunn and John Holland and his wife were among the early members of the old Mt. Vernon church. It was under the ministry of Bolivar Rudd that the present Mount Carmel church was organized in 1869, which is in direct succession from the old Mount Vernon church, and is now situated not far from where the original organization was made. It now has a nice frame building worth $800, and was dedicated by presiding elder, Wm. H. Leigh. It now has a membership of 72, with R E. Humphrey as its pastor.

BRIENSBURG CHURCH was organized in 1854, and was partly made up of the old Mount Vernon church. Rev. James Burnham and wife and Reuben Lindsey and wife were among the charter members. It now has a membership of 135, with R. E. Humphrey as its pastor.

BENTON CHURCH was organized, in the old court house, in the year 1849, with 12 charter members, embracing James Green and wife, George Green and wife, Mrs. Martha P. Ford and seven others, the officiating minister being the Rev. Sutherland. Mrs. Ford has been a member of the same church continuosly ever since and is now the only surviving charter member. In 1880 Dr. A. Smith donated the lot upon which the present church now stands, which is the first and only church ever owned by the Methodist church at Benton. The growth of this church was slow, attended with many difficulties until a few years ago. It now has a membership of 137, with Rev. T. F. Cason as its pastor. It also has an excellent Sunday School; in fact, one of the best in the county, under the guardian care of Solon L. Palmer, its popular superintendent. Among its members are the names of Judge J. J. Dupriest and wife, J. W. Dycus and wife, Dr. Van Stilley and wife, M. B. Cooper and wife, W. B. Hamilton and wife, J. D. Peterson, C. Parker, Prof. J. P. Brannock and wife, and Solon I. Palmer.

BIRMINGHAM CHURCH was organized, back in the fifties, by the Rev. Levi Lee. Elizabeth Dunn and B. Locker are the only surviving charter members. It has had three houses; the first was burned in 1868, the second was torn down to give way for a new one which was built in 1893. The new house is valued at $800, and the church at present has a membership of 43, with the Rev. Wm. B. Mathews as its pastor.

HAMLET CHURCH was organized September 10, 1893, by the Rev. J. W. Morefield, with 10 charter members; their names are as follows: J. H. Ham and wife, J. B. Roberts and wife, E. J. Jones, C. A. Belcher, G. W. Dunn, E. J. Dunn and D. H. Collie and wife. It owns no house of worship, has a membership of 11, with R. E. Humphrey as its pastor.

PALMA CHURCH is situated in the north part of the county, has a membership of 35, and the Rev. R. E. Humphrey is its pastor.

OAK LEVEL CHURCH is situated in the northwest part of the county, near the McCracken county line. It has 85 members. Rev. R. E. Humphrey, pastor.

UNION HILL church has 34 members, and its pastoral work done by the Rev. R. E. Humphrey, and owns no house.

CALVERT CITY church has not been organized many years. Wm. B. Mathews, pastor.

OLIVE church was organized several years ago. It owns no house but worships in a Union church with the Baptists. T. W. Hardin is the pastor.

MAPLE SPRINGS has an organized church, but the date of its organization is not at hand, but it owns a house, and its present pastor is T. W. Hardin.

HARDIN church was organized in the year 1892, and at present has a membership of 44, with T. F. Cason as it pastor. It owns a new house, and the success of the church is assured.

LIBERTY church is situated near Stice's School house in the eastern part of the county, owns a new house, and William B. Mathews is its pastor.

GILBERTSVILLE church has only been organized a short time, with a membership of 20. W. B. Mathews, pastor.

PLEASANT GROVE church was organized many years ago, with R. P. Finney and wife, G. W. Anderson, S. T. Green and wife, T. J. Green, Jacob Brazel, Isaac Washam, Nelson Washam and John Vaughn and wife as the charter members. It owns a house worth $500, and has 90 members. Rev. J. S. Carl has been the pastor for four years.

NEW HOPE church was organized 1827, and for many years was called Davis' Chapel. Hicks Ray, Rhoda Sutherland and Mrs. James P. Smith were among its charter members. Mrs. Smith and Hicks Ray are still living. This church has a house worth $500, and has a membership of 116, with J. S. Carl as pastor.

CHURCH GROVE church was organized 1863, at the house of George Green, when he and his wife, James Green and wife,

Lane Halton and wife, and others became charter members. It now owns a good church house and has 76 members, with J. S. Carl as its pastor.

OAK LEVEL Church was organized, in 1885, by Rev. C. D. Davis. R. Holmes and wife, R. T. Tyree and wife, E. P. Nance and wife, W. H. Nance and wife, Joel Parks and wife, and 20 others, were the charter members. This church now owns a good house worth $800, and has a membership of 107, with Rev. J. S. Carl as pastor.

SUMMARY.

From the small number in 1823, the Methodist Church has continued to grow in Marshall County, until now it has 18 organized churches, with a membership of 1,200. It owns 15 church-houses and four parsonages, valued at $10,000, and four traveling and 10 local preachers.

THE CHRISTIAN CHURCH.

This denomination had an organization near old Wadesboro, in what was then Calloway County, long before Marshall was made a separate county. The first ministers were Elder Marshall Starks and his father, and they preached and organized the first church of the kind in Western Kentucky, in about the year 1832. They did some hard work in those old pioneer times to convince the people and establish a church after the order of the original Apostolic churches that were organized in the days of the Apostles. They preached Faith, Repentance, Confession and Baptism in the order in which they appear in the New Testament. They preached their doctrine with force and power, and many believed it and obeyed the gospel, thus making a beginning for the great work that has been accomplished in this country in after years. The doctrines of the Christian Church were bitterly opposed by all the other denominations then, so much so, that a generation passed away before the people became conservative enough to hear the gospel, as it fell in burning words from the lips of these early and devout ministers of the Bible, as taught by the apostles and prophets. For over forty years its growth in this country was slow, but during the past twenty years it has kept pace with other denominations, and now it has seven well organized churches and a fast growing membership.

BENTON Church was organized by Elder J. F. Mecoy on the fourth Lord's day, May 28, 1868, with the following charter members: Joseph Meyers, and wife, Joseph F. Lee and wife, Jackson Barry and wife, Wesley Potts, A. J. Starks, J. M. P. Brewer, Tennessee I. Troutt, Mrs. Victoria J. Covington, Mrs. M. C. McElyea, Elizabeth Brewer, Mrs. I. B. Troutt T. E. Bondurant and John M. Stephens. The church never owned a house until 1894, when it purchased the interest of the Missionary Baptists, Union Church. It has been served, since its organization, by the following ministers: Wm. M. Starks, James Lindsey, J. F. Mecoy, W. L. Butler, John W. Holsapple, T. M. Matthews, and J. C. Tulley, its present popular pastor. It was organized with 16 charter members, and now has a membership of 93, with J. M. Stephens, W. A. Holland and E. Barry as its elders, and T. D. Brown and J. F. Lee, deacons, and E. Barry, clerk.

CHURCH AT FAIR DEALING.—J. W. Holsapple and wife, John Norwood, W. F. G. Collie, A. T. Sims and others met with D. L. Nelson and wife at their house on Oct. 26, 1886, to organize a Church of Christ. Twenty-eight names were enrolled. A. T. Sims and D. L. Nelson were elected elders, and John Norwood and W. F. G. Collie deacons. J. W. Holsapple, J. M. Pace, J. F. Mecoy, W. A. Utley and Jas. Ratcliffe have preached as pastors for the church. D. L. Nelson, one of the elders, has also done some preaching for the church. J. H. Thomas, J. F. Mecoy, J. W. Gant and J. W. Holsapple have held protracted meetings. The membership now numbers 51. The church owns a good frame building, situated on a beautiful cite north of the cross roads, at Fair Dealing. Here the congregation meets for worship on the second Lord's day in each month, and here is kept up a Sunday School and Bible Reading Circle. Present elders, D. L. Nelson, A. T. Sims, D. F. Rogers, J. M. Goheen and W. H. Edwards. Deacons, John Norwood, W. F. G. Collie, W. R. Anderson and Chas. W. McAtee. D. L. Nelson is now doing the monthly preaching. The church contributes to all missionary enterprises. Hugh Brown, W. F. G. Collin and D. L. Nelson, trustees.

CHURCH AT SHARPE was organized several years ago, and is situated in the northwest part of the county, in a good farming country. It owns a house of worship and has a membership of about 40, and Elder J. R. Hill, of Murray, is its present pastor.

OAK LEVEL church was organized about 1886, by Elder J. W. Holsapple. It now has a membership of about 40, and owns a beautiful church house. Elder Holsapple preached the first sermon ever delivered in Oak Level.

CALVERT CITY church was organized in 1893, by Elder J. R. Hill. It worships in a Union church with the Methodists, and has 30 members. Elder Hill is its present pastor.

UNION HILL church is what was once Liberty church that was organize, away back in the forties, by Wm. Marshall Starks and his father. This is one of the oldest churches in the country. It has a new house and a membership of about 250. Elder J. R. Hill is its present pastor.

BRIENSBURG church was originally organized at the residence of Elder James Lindsey, with himself and wife, his son Wm. and wife, his son James and wife, and his daughter Miss Polly Lindsey, afterwards the wife of Jack Finch. This organization remained at the home of Elder James Lindsey for some time, and he continued to preach once a month until the number increased sufficiently to build a house, when they all joined themselves together on certain days and cut down trees and hauled the logs and built them a plain log house in which to worship. It was in this crude structure that Union church was organized, over fifty years ago. It became a power for good, and it grew in numbers and in influence until it was the largest organized religious congregation in the county. James Lindsey, James R. Jones and John F. Mecoy were the elders that preached the Word for so many years with such power in Old Union church. The members became so numerous and were scattered over such a broad territory that the leaders in the church saw the necessity of building a larger and better house, in a more accessible and convenient place, and about 15 years ago a new house was built in the town of Briensburg, in which now worships the true succession of the Old Union congregation, and it is now known and called the Briensburg church. It has a membership of about 350, and Elder J. R. Hill, of Murray, is its present pastor. An effort was made to get a full and complete history of this large and prosperous congregation, from the time of its earliest organization down to the present time, but it failed.

THE MISSIONARY BAPTIST CHURCH.

This denomination was not among the earliest organized churches in the county, but soon after Marshall county became independent and separate from Calloway county the Missionary Baptists began to work in different parts of the county, and locate here and there, preparatory to organizing themselves into separate churches. Efforts were made to get a full and complete history of the first organized Baptist church in the county, but to some extent they were unsuccessful, yet they are given as accurate as the information at hand will justify. The organization began about 1844, and from that day down to the present the Missionary Baptists have kept pace with the other denominations in the county, and now it has twelve organized working churches with a membership of 931 in good standing. Below can be found the names of all the churches, the number of communicants and the names of their present pastors:

BENTON church was organized October 4, 1860, by Elders Lowery McClain, James Morton and D. M. Green, with Mrs. Geraldine H. Wilson, Elizabeth Finley, E. Crow and wife, Martha Thompson, Rachael Green, Martha Green, M. C. Rowland, Elizabeth Hanks and Lucinda Bourland as charter members, and only four of whom are now living. With these ten persons the church struggled along through the war, and for many years afterward without much increase in its membership or religious enthusiasm. For 34 long years it never owned a house of its own, but from 1882 to 1894 it held a half interest in the Union church and worshiped with the members of the Christian church. Early in 1894 it sold its interest to the Christian brethren for $450, and during the same year built a new house of its own at a cost of $2,000. It was dedicated November 18, 1894, by J. W. Warder, of Louisville, Ky. It now has a membership of 80 with Dr. B. T. Hall as pastor.

OLIVE church was organized in 1847, and has never owned a house of its own, but is now jointly worshiping in a house owned by it and the Methodist church. It now has 74 members and is under the pastoral care of Elder J. P. Tubbs.

PLEASANT HOPE church was organized at Cap Spring, near Fair Dealing, 1867, with Caleb Lindsey and wife, John Lindsey and wife and several others as charter members. The old house went down several years ago and a new one was built on the Fair Dealing and Birmingham road, and it was named Pleasant Hope. It now owns a good house with a membership of 106 and Elder J. P. Tubbs as pastor.

BETHLEHEM church was organized in 1844, and is said to be the oldest Missionary Baptist church in the county. It was originally situated about two miles west of Calvert City, on the Benton and Calvert City road, but a few years ago a new house was built near the old State road and just back of the W. C. Staton farm and within one mile of Coy. It owns a new house, has 70 members and is preached for by Eld. I. E. Wallace.

ZION'S CAUSE church was organized in 1885, near Palma, and it has 59 members and is a prosperous young church.

HARDIN church was organized in 1893, in a new and beautiful house, at Hardin, by Elder N. S. Castleberry, who is its present pastor. The church has 21 members and will soon have a membership much larger. Mr. Hardin Irvan, an old and influential citizen, gave $500 towards the erection of the new house.

NEW ZION church was organized 1892, in the southwest part of the county, near Magness, and it now has a membership of 67.

NEW BETHEL church, located four miles west of Benton, on the Benton and Mayfield road, was organized in 1854. It owns a house, has a membership of 58, and Dr. B. T. Hall is its present pastor.

NEW HARMONY is located six miles west of Benton, was organized in 1867, has a membership of 133, and it now has Elder I. E. Wallace for its pastor.

GILBERTSVILLE church was organized at Gilbertsville in 1893, by Elder D. M. Green, and now has 22 members.

CALVERT CITY church is located in Calvert City, and was organized in 1878, and now has 123 members. Elders I. E. Wallace, D. M. Green and N. S. Castleberry have labored as its pastors for a number of years.

BETHEL church is located in the northeast part of the county, near the Stice school house. It owns a new house and also has a membership of 121. It was organized over 30 years ago and is the succession of Bethel church that existed and was located near the Lents place almost a generation ago.

UNION RIDGE church is located near Aurora and was organized in 1881. It has a membership of 40 and Elder J. P. Tubbs is its popular and conscientious pastor.

CHURCH SUMMARY.

The following figures show the relative strength of the various churches in Marshall county January 1, 1895: Cumberland Presbyterians, 225; Primitive Baptists, 263; Methodist Church South, 1,203; Missionary Baptists, 931; Christian Church, 825. Total, 3,447.

Historical Church Notes.

The first Christian church organized this side of the Tennessee river was organized by Elder Reuben Starks, father of Wm Marshall Starks, at old Liberty in June, 1832. These are the charter members: Reuben Starks and wife, Jesse Starks and wife and his daughter, who is now the aged wife of Uncle Jarrett Haymes, Daniel Pace and wife and Langston Pace. Mrs. Haymes is the only one of the charter members now living.

Secret Societies.

The first lodge of any secret society organized in this county was Benton Lodge No. 205, Ancient York Masons. It was established in 1849 in one of the upper rooms of the then new court house. It was organized by Reuben Rowland, Peter W. Gardner, George Miller and others, and continued to meet in the court house for some time, but afterwards began holding its meetings up stairs in the old Union church, where it continued to meet until the charter of the lodge was surrendered in 1882, to the Grand Lodge of the State.

KNIGHTS OF HONOR—Marshall Lodge No. 681, Knights of Honor, was organized September 3, 1878, in one of the rooms up stairs in the old court house, with the following named charter members and officers: E. Barry, W. A. Holland, J. M. Stilley, J. F. Brandon, W. J. Wilson, T. L. Goheen, jr., G. W. Brandon, M. C. Rowland and D. G. Smith. The lodge is still in existence.

Benton Lodge, Odd Fellows, No. 282, was organized April 7, 1888, in the room up stairs over Cooper's store, where it still meets.

Sweet Retreat lodge, No. 1363, I. O. G. T., was organized by J. J. Hickman, 1872, in the Marshall County Seminary. The lodge continued to meet there for some time, then for many years up stairs in the old court house, and after many years of usefulness it went down, and now there is no Good Templar's lodge here.

There was a lodge organized here many years ago called the Oriental Order of Humility. It lasted for a short time, but is now extinct. There is, however, a lodge of the same kind in good working order near Aurora.

MASONIC LODGES.—At present there are but three working Masonic lodges in the county; one at Calvert City, one at Olive and one at Briensburg. These are the only ones that have stood the wreck of Masonic lodges in Marshall county during the past fifteen years. Benton lodge No. 205, received a dispensation prior to August, 1849, but it was renewed August, 1849, and chartered August, 1850, with Reuben Rowland its first Master, and in 1858 it had 37 members, and when it went down in 1882, there were 76 members.

FARMERS AND LABORERS UNION.—About six years ago there were many Wheeler and Alliance lodges organized in Marshall county. They were organized at nearly all the school houses in the country. Men and women, both, were admitted to membership. The objects of these orders were to better the condition of the laboring classes. These two organizations, whose principles were about the same, united under the name of the Farmers and Laborers Union. There are State unions, District and county sub-unions. Quite a number of these unions have gone down, but at present the following sub-unions are still in working order, with the following membership; Salem, 28; Altona, 12; Enterprise, 37; Cypress Creek, 31; Griggs, 31; Briensburg, 25; Oak Valley, 56; Lee Grove, 24; Church Grove, 50; Oak Hill, 14; and Howards Grove, 27. The total membership at present in the county is 335, in the 11 lodges that are now in existence. It is thought that the organization and promulgation of these orders have made the radical changes in the political complexion that has taken place in the minds of the voters of Marshall county.

Bits of Odd History.

The first regular court held in the county was under an harbor in the public square, in September 1842. Everyone present, except five were in their shirt sleeves.

Musters were held in the olden times, about six times each year; Company, four times; battalion, one; regimental, one. There have been no musters held in this county since the war.

The first corn raised in the county was by Johnathan Grear, at the mouth of Jonathan's Creek, in the year 1818.

There have been two elections held by the people to move the county seat from Benton, but both were unsuccessful. The first was held in August, 1843, to remove it to Briensburg; the second in August, 1876, to carry it from its present site to Birmingham. But since the building of the new court house the question of county seat removal is forever settled.

A beautiful Banner was given the county in 1856 as the county casting the biggest democratic majority of any county in this Congressional district; but the county would hardly be so lucky at the present time.

Horse Stealing in 1844-5 was carried on very extensively in this section of the country, by Alonzo Pennington, who was the leader of a dangerous gang of horse thieves, with his headquarters about two miles from Benton. He and most of his gang were afterwards caught, and some of them sent to the penitentiary, but Pennington, himself, was hung in Hopkinsville, in May, 1846, for murder.

Marriage Licenses.—Since the organization of the county there have been 4,354 marriage license issued. The first license was issued by Henry Hand, for John T. Grubbs to Miss Velina Duncan, and they were married by Henry Darnall on October 25, 1842.

Antiquities.—From Collins' History we learn that near Brewer's Mills, in the southwest part of the county, are the remains of an Indian town, and that on a hill at the Bird Griffith place, four miles northwest of Benton are a mound and Indian burying ground, where human remains, shells, stone vessels and other curious implements can be found in abundance. There are a few mounds in the county that mark the path of the Mound Builders, a race of people of which we know but little.

Curiosities.—Three miles from Calvert City there is a mineral spring whose waters contain sulphurated hydrogen, carbonic acid gas, sulphate and chloride of lime, magnesia and iron. This water is fine for invalids, and if known, would be as famous as the great Dawson water. It is situated on Big Cypress, near Mrs. Joe Greer's. A sink hole, or small lake, for it is filled with water, three miles south of Benton, on a high hill, has an unknown depth. The water in it neither rises or falls and is on a level 50 feet above the bed of a creek near by.

Few Words About the Late Lamented
GEORGE W. LOCKER.

George W. Locker was born in Trigg county, Ky., November 26, 1851. Died at his home in Birmingham, Ky., August 7, 1894. He was educated in the common schools of his day, but being a boy of energy and great natural ability, he received a better English education than most boys of like opportunities. His parents were poor, and when he arrived at manhood, he was also a young man without any of this world's goods, but he was not long to remain so. He began business as one of the firm of Locker, Kinsolving & Co., but it was not long until he commenced business for himself, and in his own name. He was married to Miss Hellen M. Long, September 11, 1878, at Eddyville, Ky. Only one child blessed this union, "Freddie," who died in its infancy. May the 9th, 1894, he formed a co-partnership in business with his brother-in-law, John E. Long, and the business is now conducted under the name of Locker & Long. He was a devout member of the Methodist church, and in politics an unflinching and uncompromising republican. He was the most successful business man in the county, and his friends were numbered by the score. He left a wife, who in life was tender, kind and true, and in death she has never forsaken him.

School Interest of the County.

The common school interests began with the organization of the county, and as the interests grew in the state so it has grown in the county. When the county was organized the state drew six per cent interest from the United States government on $850,000, which was proportioned on a per capita basis to all the counties in the state, and this was all the revenue for school purposes from 1838 to 1849. In 1849 the people of the state voted two cents on the $100 worth of property for school purposes, which was added to the amount received as interest from the National government, which constituted the school fund until 1855, when a three cents additional tax was voted. In 1869 fifteen cents more was voted, and in 1882 another two cents tax was added by a vote of the people, which made a total of 22 cents on the $100 worth of property, that is now collected for school purposes in the state. There are other resources from which the school fund is increased, besides the 22 cents property tax. It is increased by drawing six per cent interest on $1,327,000 worth of bonds, and also by dividends arising from a bank stock of $73,500. The other resources arise from a surplus due the counties of the state of $381,906.08 from which interest is collected. The school fund is also augmented by interest on $606,641.03 received from the United States government in 1892, and on license forfeitures, fines, etc.

The above is a true statement of the resources from which the school fund is now made up in Kentucky. The total amount of the school fund in 1894 was about two million dollars. In 1860 there were 4,696 common school districts in the state, with 286,370 pupil children, and a per capita of 70 cents; in 1871 there were 5,177 districts with 389,836 pupil children and a per capita of $2; in 1880 there were 6,177 districts with 478,554 pupil children and a per capita of $1.25; in 1890 there were 6,775 districts with 565,470 pupil children and a per capita of $2.15; in 1894 there were 8,042 school districts, counting as one district all towns of the first four classes, with 720,000 pupil children, and a per capita of $2.75. Marshall county has 54 districts for white and two for colored children, with a total of

4,094 white pupil children, and 151 colored pupil children. The school fund distributed in 1894 to the white children of Marshall county amounted to $11,497.59, and $421.29 to the teachers of the colored schools. The per capita for the school year ending June 30, 1894, was $2.85, the largest amount ever drawn in the state.

The schools are in better condition now than ever before in the county. In over half of the districts the people have provided themselves with good school houses and good seats. This has been done by local taxation. Each district has a good five months school, taught each year, in which children between the ages of six and twenty have free access. The class of teachers has greatly improved in recent years as well as the conveniences for the pupil. The teachers are better paid for their services now than they were many years ago, besides they now get their pay at the end of each month, which enables them to better meet their obligations and live like men and women worthy of their calling. The schools of the county are looked after and cared for by that great friend to popular education, Louis Wallace, the present county superintendent.

Below can be found the name and number of each school district in the county, together with the name of the teacher for the year 1894.

1. Walnut Grove—W M Anderson
2. Alford—L A Robb.
3. Unity—R L Nanney.
4. Joppa—D W Lents.
5. Olive—Mollie Treas.
6. Johnson District—S T Harrison
8. Collie District—R W West.
9. Cleveland—A E Cross.
10. Maple Springs—T D Brown.
11. Salem—Charlie Jones.
13. Birmingham—B M Philley.
14. Mt. Carmel—Jane Holland.
15. White Oak—Ida Luter.
16. Clark—M B Pace.
17. Briensburg—John T Draffen.
18. Stice—L V Henson.
19. Oak Ridge—E G Maddox.
20. Gilbertsville—G C Edwards.
21. Pugh—E L Sargent.
22. Stahl—T I Hartsfield.
23. Scale—U G Karnes.
24. Griggs—L O Peck.
25. Palma—Naomi Reeves.
26. McCain—A T Willoughby.
27. Calvert City—Moffit Howard.
28. Altona—Mamie Johnson.
29. Howard's Grove—D V Sims.
30. Lone Valley—L L Freeman.
31. Staton's—W H Elliott.
32. Oak Hill—J N Holland.
33. Sharpe C H Hamilton.
34. Stringtown Maggie Hill.
35. Hickory Grove D B Crowell.
36. New Harmony H B Holland.
37. Brazzeel Dora Kelley.
38. Benton J P Brannock.
39. Church Grove Elihu Harris.
40. Cherry Grove J D Mathis.
41. Pleasant Valley J M Houser.
42. Oak Level J N Henson.
43. Johnson Bethel Hall.
44. Pleasant Grove L I Bean.
45. Darnall E W Stone.
46. Liberty H W Jones.
47. Hardin Thos Jackson.
48. Jackson Wm Barnhart.
49. Phipps F A Higgins.
50. Hale Spring Edna Starks.
51. Beasley George W Oliver.
52. Smith's Attie Houston.
53. Davis Chapel J T Clark.
54. Lucas Holland's Floy Heath.
55. Coursey J M McGee.
56. Cope M A Bearden.

THE MARSHALL COUNTY SEMINARY

This important institution of learning is located in the town of Benton, and is the property of the county. It was located where it now is on February 3, 1868, by a board of trustees, consisting of T. L. Goheen, sr., W. C. Holland, J. H. Johnston, Josiah Wood, Samual Mathis, C. Parker and J. W. Whitnel. The land vested in them for seminary purposes embraced nine quarter sections in Graves county, 1,440 acres, all of which has been sold and expended in building, repairing and keeping up the seminary, except $484.41, the amount now on hand. The sum of money that has been received from these lands amounts to over $10,000, which has been a great blessing to the people of the county in furnishing them an institution of learning in which to educate their sons and daughters. The Seminary was consolidated with common school district No. 38, in 1888, by an act of the Legislature, which enables the people living in the Benton district to use it for common school purposes. The trustees are appointed for life, or during good behavior. The present board is compased of J. H. Johnston, W. C. Holland, C. Parker, J. H. Strow, W. A. Holland, J. M. Fisher and J. R. Lemon; the first four named having served continuously for over 26 years. The first teacher was Prof. A. Pomroy, with W. T. Shelton assistant, and the present principal is Prof. J. P. Brannock, with Miss Mary Holland and Miss Lucy Bearden assistants. The Seminary property is now worth about $6,000.

THE FIRST FREE SCHOOL

Ever taught in Marshall county was taught at old Liberty Church, this side of Wadesboro, by Wm. Thompson, in the year 1845, with Uncle Jarett Haymes as one of the trustees. There were three commissioners then, Daniel Pace, Rev. Hugh Gilbert and Hardin Stone. The examiners were P. Palmer and Henry Hand. Hope Pace and wife, J. C. Gilbert, John H. Strow and Spencer Cope were some of the pupils that attended that school.

JARRETT HAYMES

Was the first school trustee that was ever elected in Marshall county. He was born in Virginia, April 29, 1808; Came to Todd county, Kentucky, 1820; Moved to near where he now lives in 1825, and was married to Miss Nancy Starks, a sister of Marshall Starks, January 26, 1836. Both are yet living and are hearty and active.

J. J. DUPRIEST, County Judge.
(For Sketch see page 80.)

JOHN T. DRAFFEN.

John T. Draffen was born in Marshall county, Ky., on March 10, 1857; moved with his father to Symsonia, Graves county,

Kentucky, on February 18, 1861. Came up under many disadvantages, parents poor, but honest, neither could read or write. Educated in the country schools of that day. Examined for a teachers certificate on July 5, 1879, securing a first-class, first grade; getting the best grade of the 11 who were then examined. Has been teaching continuously in the public schools ever since. Began reading law at home in June, 1891; was examined in June, 1893, obtaining a license to practice in the courts of this commonwealth. Made an unsuccessful race for the Democratic nomination for Judge of the Marshall County Court in 1894. Was married on February 3, 1889, to Miss Emma Styers, in the old church at Slabtown, Graves county, Ky., after which he moved to Marshall county, where he has made his home since. He was examined by the county board of examiners in July, 1893, when he obtained a first-class certificate, general average being 90.4, which was said to have been the hardest examination ever held in the State. Was appointed one of school examiners for Marshall county by L. E. Wallace, county commissioner, in August, 1894. He is now teaching the public school in Briensburg district, No. 17, which will expire in December 1894. He and his wife are both members of the M. E. Church South, and he is a true democrat. Mr. Draffen is one of the coming men of his county.

ROBERT L. SHEMWELL.

Robert L. Shemwell was born March 14, 1865, two miles south of Oak Level, Marshall county, Kentucky. He is the tenth and youngest child of David A. and Permelia J. Shemwell, and was raised on a farm and sent to the common schools of his neigh-

R. L. SHEMWELL.

borhood until he was 24 years old, when he entered Smith's Business College, at Lexington, Ky., at which he graduated April 9, 1889. He returned home and began the profession of teaching school, and continued until he had taught 40 months, and retired from the profession in 1891. In 1889 he began the study of law under the Hon. W. M. Reed, and was admitted to the bar as a licensed attorney in 1890. In 1892 he was nominated by the democratic party for Circuit Court Clerk, and made the race against M. N. Sims, the nominee of the people's party. He received 1019 votes, and Sims 702; being elected by 317 majority. He qualified January 1, 1893, and his term of office will expire January 1, 1898. He is a democrat, belongs to no church or secret society and weighs 275 pounds. He is clever, social and polite and is one of the most popular men in the county.

E. W. STONE.

E. W. Stone, one of the brightest young men and most successful teachers in the county, was born in Marshall county, Kentucky in 1867, in the eastern part of the county near Birmingham. He is the oldest son of John P. and Ellen Stone. He was raised on a farm and educated in the schools of Cap Spring, Church Grove and the Marshall County Seminary. He is at present teaching in district No. 45, and holds a first-class certificate. He began teaching when he was 21 years old, but has not given

all of his time to that profession, yet he has taught 25 months of common schools. He spent a short time in the drug business at Birmingham, and in the general merchandise business at Fair Dealing. He is a young man of good character, well stocked in common sense, and a teacher of the best grade. If no misfortune overtakes him he is destined to be one of the leading young men of the county.

A. T. JACKSON.

A. T. JACKSON.

A. T. Jackson was born June 30, 1864, in the northern part of Calloway county. He is a son of G. W. and Elizabeth Jackson; was raised on a farm and educated in the common schools of the county, except four months he attended the Murray Institute. He began teaching school at Phipps' school house in Marshall county in 1886, and with the exception of 1890, has taught every year since. He is now the popular teacher in the Hardin district, at the end of which term he will have taught a total of 65 months. With the exception of one school he has always taught with a first-class certificate. Prof Jackson is truly a self-made man, and deserves much credit for his advancement in the cause of education. He is an unmarried man and a firm believer in the doctrines of the peoples party.

JAS. N. HOLLAND

is of Scotch-Irish descent and is the son of J. L. and Mary Holland; was born near Birmingham, Marshall county, in Jan. 1869. He was raised on a farm, and, like most country boys, his early education was to some extent neglected, but in 1889 he entered the Birmingham school, and while there under the care of J. G. Lovett

he began to lay the foundation of a good English education. In

1891 he attended the Marshall County Seminary, at Benton; in the latter part of the same year he assisted J. G. Lovett in district No. 8, in 1892 he again attended school at Birmingham, but in the fall of the same year he was employed as teacher in district No. 8- where he taught a very interesting school. In January, 1893, he entered the Murray Institute, and after attending one session he taught at Maple Springs, perhaps the best school since the days of J. W. Holsapple. Early in the year 1894 he made an unsuccessful race for the democratic nomination for county clerk. In March, 1894, he again entered the Murry Institute, at the close of which, he was employed in the common school at Oak Hill, where he is now teaching with a first-class certificate. He is a close student, a deep thinker, and a fluent speaker. He is one of the coming young men of the county.

LEON LEWIS FREEMAN

One of the bright young teachers of the county, was born August 28, 1873, in the north part of Marshall county, Kentucky.

He attended the common schools in his home district No. 30 until January 1891, when he entered that most excellent school at Lebanon, Ohio, where he remained until he completed his business course in the following June. In 1892 he taught his first school in district No. 28, at Altona; in 1893 he taught at Gilbertsville, and is now teaching a satisfactory school at Lone Valley, his home district. His first examination was in 1889, while M. B. Pace was commissioner and W. M. Anderson and T. D. Brown examiners. He has held a good certificate all the time since, the general average at his last examination reaching 84. He is moral, studious and energetic, and at no distant day will be a man of influence and a prominent educator.

WILLIAM H. ELLIOTT

Was born in the southeast part of the county January 8, 1860, of poor parentage. He is a son of John and Matilda Elliott. His father died when he was two, and his mother when he was  in his fifth year. Being left an orphan boy he lived with his relatives until he was eight years old, when he went to live with the Rev. Elisha Luter, where he lived and attended the common schools during the remainder of his boyhood. After he quit the common schools he attended school at Woodville, Bowling Green, Ky., and Valparaiso, Ind. The best part of his education he acquired at home under adverse circumstances. He has been teaching school since 1882, since which time he has taught 88 months of schools; joined the M. E. church at Mt. Carmel 1883, but his membership is now at Oakland; he is also a member of the Labor Union; he has one State and four first-class county certificates, the general average of the last one 92.5, and taught in district No. 31 in 1894, with 86 pupils. He has always been energetic, sober and economical, and is now the owner of a good home worth $2,000. He has one sister, Mrs. Belle Roberts, of Dallas, Texas, and one brother, John R. Elliott, now of West Kentucky, and his uncle, Prof. T. N. Elliott, of Forreston, Texas, who is one of the prominent educators of that state. There is no better teacher or citizen in the county than Prof. William Henry Elliott.

The Medical Profession.

The medical profession in Marshall county is represented by the following named practicing physicians, who are authorized to practice medicine in the county, under the late laws of the state:

Dr. E. G. Thomas, born in Mayfield, Ky., 42 years ago, graduated in the medical department of the University of Louisville March 11, 1873.

Dr. Van A. Stilley, born in Calloway county, Ky., 28 years ago, and graduated in the University of Louisville February 28, 1890.

Dr. William S. Stone, born in Calloway county, Ky., February 22, 1862, and graduated in the medical department of the University of Louisville March 1, 1888.

Dr. T. B. Helm was born in Marshall county, Ky., November 7, 1870; graduated in the Kentucky School of Medicine, Louisville, Ky., June 1893.

Dr. J. M. Woodall was born in Marshall county, Ky; is 23 years old and graduated in the medical department of the University of Louisville, Ky., March 13, 1893.

Dr. E. A. Henson is 51 years old and graduated at University at Nashville and Vanderbuilt University Nashville. Tennessee, on March 25, 1890.

Dr. Charles E. Howard is 29 years old, born in Hickman county, Ky., and graduated at the University of Louisville, May 14, 1892.

Dr. A. H. Freeman was born in Marshall county, Ky., 28 years ago, and graduated at the Kentucky School of Medicine Louisville, Ky., June 20, 1892.

Dr. B. B. Griffeth was born in Ballard county, Ky., 33 years ago and graduated in the Missouri Medical College, St. Louis, Mo., March 4, 1884.

Dr. R. M. Jones was born in Bath county, Ky., 36 years ago and graduated in the Kentucky School of Medicine, Louisville, Ky., June 28, 1889.

Dr. Rufus H. Starks was born in Marshall county, Ky., 42 years ago and graduated at the Louisville Medical College, Louisville, Ky., February 27, 1878.

Dr. L. E. Finley was born in Trigg county, Ky., 41 years ago and graduated in the Kentucky School of Medicine, June 20, 1889.

Dr. Horace N. Robertson was born in Marshall county, Ky., 24 years ago and graduated in the Kentucky School of Medicine Louisville, Ky., June 20, 1891.

Dr. T. C. Coleman was born in Calloway county, Ky., 40 years ago and graduated in the medical department of the Vanderbuilt University, Nashville, Tenn., March 1884.

Dr. B. T. Hall was born in Graves county, Ky., 42 years ago and graduated at the Eclectic Medical Institute, Cincinnati, Ohio, May 9, 1876.

Dr. Samuel Graham is 71 years old, was born in Chatham county, Georgia, and is one of the old common practitioners of medicine.

Dr. J. M. Mooney was born in Tennessee, is 66 years old and is authorized to practice medicine under the old law.

Dr. J. B. Wilson was born in Kentucky, 67 years ago, and is a regular practitioner under the old law.

Dr. Thomas E. Russell was born in Calloway county, 31 years ago and graduated in the medical department of the University of Louisville, March 1886.

Dr. John W. Pendley was born in Hopkins county, Ky., 33 years ago and graduated in the Memphis Hospital Medical College, March 1893.

Dr. J. A. Jones was born in Bedford county, Tenn., 37 years ago and is practicing under a certificate from the State Board of Health.

Dr. Ben T. Frank was born 49 years ago in Owen county, Kentucky, and graduated at the Miami Medical College, Cincinnati, Ohio, March 1, 1867.

Dr. E. C. Dycus, was born in Hart county, Kentucky, 73 years ago, and now practices medicine under a certificate under the law of 1874 and 1878. And is one of the oldest in the county.

There were but few physicians in the county in its early history, and those that were here underwent many hardships and exposures. The settlements were few and far between, and the men who did the practice in those days were compelled to make many long and lonesome trips. Doctors Justice and Ab Shinn were among the physicians back in the forties. Later on Dr. R. Nuckolls was a conspicuous character in the profession. Brian, Penner, Dycus, Irvan, Lackey, Miller and Holland were among the physicians who began the practice of medicine in the early history of the county. There are now 23 regular physicians in the county.

JOSEPH M. MOONEY, M. D.

Dr. Joseph M. Mooney was born in East Tennessee, March 20, 1828. Came with his parents to Henry county, in the west-

ern part of the state, 1840, where he remained until 1851, when he came to Calloway county, Kentucky, but on January 13, 1850, he was married to Miss Julia A. Dunn, of Henry county, Tennessee. He came to Marshall county in 1865, and located at Briensburg, where he yet resides. His second marriage was to Mrs. Mary A. Poiner on February 10, 1881. Six children blessed the first union, and two the second. He joined the Methodist church in 1840, and began to preach in 1844, and is an able minister now, though he gives most of his time to his profession. He studied medicine under Holt & Graves and began to practice in 1860. He joined the Masonic fraternity at Paris, Tennessee, in 1855, since which time he has become a well-informed Mason in the Blue Lodge, Chapter and Council. He was raised on a farm, and his educational advantages were very poor, but by his energy he became a man of wonderful information.

WM. SPEER STONE, M. D.

Dr. William Speer Stone was born February 22, 1862, in Calloway county, Kentucky. His father, John W. Stone, and his  mother were both born in Tennessee. His mother was Miss Lottie M. Speer. His father was a fine mechanic and was the inventor of Stone's Patent Excelsior Tobacco Plug Machine, patented May 17, 1870. The subject of this sketch was raised on a farm, and educated in the common schools of Calloway county. He began the study of medicine in 1882 under his brother, Dr J. F. Stone; attended the medical department of the University of Louisville, 1883-4; began the practice of medicine at Shiloh, Calloway county in 1884, but at the close of the same year he moved to Fair Dealing, Marshall county. He graduated in medicine March 1888, returned home and moved to Birmingham in 1891, where he is now engaged in the practice of his profession. He was married May 17, 1888, to Miss N. E. Risenhoover. He joined the M. E. church in 1888; is a Mason, and a sound democrat. He is very popular where he resides both as a skilled physician and a gentleman of honor and integrity.

THOS. B. HELM.

Dr. Thomas B. Helm was born near Palma, Marshall county, Ky., Nov. 7, 1870. He is a son of J. M. Helm, who was one of the county's prominent men in his day. He was raised on a farm and educated in the common schools  of the county, and when he grew to manhood he began the study of medicine under Dr. B. T. Hall. In January, 1892, he entered the Kentucky School of Medicine at Louisville, and in June, 1893, graduated with becoming honors. He returned to his home and began the practice of his profession at Oak Level where he now resides. He is a young man, unmarried, a member of no church or secret society, but is a democrat in all that the word means.

ALBERT HOWARD FREEMAN, M. D  was born July 3, 1866, on a farm near Palma. He is the oldest child of Henry and Catherine Freeman. During his boyhood days he went to the public schools in winter and worked on the farm in summer, utilizing the noon rest, night and odd hours in reading and study. At the age of 17 he taught his first school; in the spring of 1884 attended the Murray Institute, teaching in the fall and winter, and again the next year. In 1886–7 he attended the National Normal University at Lebanon, Ohio, where he completed the Teacher's Course, receiving a diploma for same, then began the Scientific Course, but was compelled to leave college, when only half through, for want of money to continue, only being able to stay this long by doing janitor work for his tuition. In the fall of 1887 taught school. In October, 1888, went to Texas, where for two years he was engaged as an attendant at the North Texas Hospital for the Insane, at Terrell. Here he began the study of medicine. Returning to Kentucky he was in attendance on the lectures at the University of Louisville, 1890–91. Taught in fall of 1891. In the spring of 1892 he attended the Kentucky School of Medicine, graduating from that institution in 1892. Locating at Briensburg, where he now resides, he began the practice of his profession in July of the same year. On August 3, 1893, he was married to Miss May V. Wills, at Lawrence, Texas. They have one child, a boy, Henry, born May 31, 1894. Dr. Freeman is the present Secretary–Treasurer of the Marshall County F. & L. U., and a member of the Marshall County Medical Society, and will eventually hold many places of honor and trust among his fellows.

A Modest Christian Soldier.

ELD. J. P. TUBBS.

Elder James P. Tubbs was born a few miles east of Benton, November 3, 1847; was raised on a farm without hardly any educational advantages, and grew to manhood without any qualifications save a good physical constitution and a mind above the average in force and power. In 1862 he joined the Methodist Church South and remained with that denomination until May, 1885, when he withdrew and attached himself to the Missionary Baptist church of which he is still a member. Immediately after he became a member of the Baptist church he began to preach, but was not ordained as a full gospel minister until February 12, 1889. He was ordained by Elders N. S. Castleberry, J. H. Powell and J. E. Kelley. He has preached from 468 texts, baptized 51, and married 31 couples. Was married to Elzada L. Gregory November 22, 1866, and seven girl children have been born to them, five of whom are now living and two dead. One died at the age of four years, eight months and 16 days, the other 23 years, eight months and 10 days; the latter was a member of the church. All of the children are members of the church except the youngest one, which is now ten years old. He has been pastor of Olive church since 1889; was pastor at Birmingham 1890-91, and until he resigned his pastorship during 1891. He is a member and the pastor of Pleasant Hope church, for which he has served as its pastor during the years 1889-90-91 and 1894. Has served as pastor of Union Ridge church since 1892, and is now pastor for Ledbetter church. He is also a member of the Labor Union lodge. He was always a sober, honest, pious christian gentleman, and no man is held in higher estimation as a christian minister than the subject of this sketch.

HARDIN M. WADE.

H. M. Wade was born Jan. 29, 1842, one mile south of where Oak Level now stands. His father died in 1843, and in 1847 his mother was married to R. McCain, hence the subject of our sketch was raised by a step-father. He was raised on the farm and of course in those days had no educational advantages until 1860 he was away at school for one year, but upon his return he had a misunderstanding with his step-father and in July 1861 he joined the Confederate army, Company G., Third Kentucky Volunteers, where he remained until the early part of 1865. He was wounded August 5th, 1862, at Baton Rouge, La., by being shot through both thighs. Soon after he returned from the war he was married to Miss Samuella Tilghman, who has been dead for many years. At this time Mr. Wade was an intelligent young man, fresh from the rebel army, with a reputation for deeds of daring and bravery on the battlefields, and in 1867 he was elected Sheriff of Marshall county by a good majority over both of his opponents. He was delegate to the Appellate convention that was held in Hopkinsville in 1868 at which William Lindsay was nominated. He laid the plan by which Ed Crossland was elected to Congress. He did some work on the old Paducah Herald, Tobacco Plant, and in 1891 began the publication of the Wickliffe Enterprise. Has always been a democrat, and has been active in the politics of his country.

H. M. WADE.

STEPHEN A. WHALE.

The subject of this sketch was born March 1, 1862, in Pittsburgh, Penn., where he was educated in the common schools of that city. As soon as he was old enough he began to assist his father at his trade, which was that of a brick maker. Later on he worked in the glass works of that city, but in 1879 he came with his father to Trigg county, Ky., where he remained

S. A. WHALE.

on a farm for four years, when he left and returned to Pittsburgh, where he engaged in the fruit and vegetable business for two years. He then returned to Kentucky and located at Aurora, Marshall county. He was married August 1, 1886, to Mrs. N. A. Eggner, with whom he has lived happily ever since. He has been engaged in the business of general merchandise since 1886; in 1887 he was elected Justice of the Peace to fill out the unexpired term of R. Henderson. He was appointed to the same office in 1892 which office will expire January 1, 1895. He has been on the fiscal court for five years, and has made a safe and conservative officer. He is of German descent a Catholic in religion and a true democrat in politics. He is one of the county's best citizens.

ANOTHER ONE OF OUR MAGISTRATES.

Felix A. Arant was born in Marshall county, December 9, 1853; attended the common schools of his neighborhood when a boy, and completed his education at the Marshall County Seminary in 1874. Was married to Miss Alzada E. Fookes, December 19, 1876, by Elder Thomas F. Harrison. Seven children have blessed this union. He has lived in the northwest part of the county from his birth down to the present time. He joined the Regular Baptist church September 1881, and for years has been a deacon in his church. Was elected Justice of the Peace in 1890, and qualified in June 1891, and his term of office will expire January 1, 1895. He was raised on a farm and has always been a hard worker, and it has been by his industry and economy that he is now the owner of 278 acres of good land, 200 acres cleared and in cultivation, with good houses and plenty of stock. In 1893 he raised 750 bushels of corn, 35 tons of hay, 295 bushels of wheat, and 10,000 pounds tobacco. He is now 40 years old, was never out of the state, and has only been in four counties. He is an old-time democrat.

ARCHIBALD HUGH WEAR.

Archibald Hugh Wear, of Murray, Ky., was born in the state of Alabama, at the place now known as Tuscumbia, October 14, 1818. Went with his parents to Howard county, Missouri, about the year 1820. They only remained there about one year, moving to Montgomery county, Tennessee. In December, 1822, they moved to Marshall (then Calloway) county, Ky., and settled four miles west of Wadesboro, where the subject of this sketch was brought up on a farm. At his majority he located in Wadesboro, where he remained until 1842, when the county was divided, when he came to Benton and purchased the property which is now owned by Brandon Brothers, but afterwards sold his property to Mr. Willis Strow, and went to Murray, or rather where Murray was to be. He helped lay off and locate the town, and was one of the first men to sleep in the town, which consisted then of one log cabin. He has resided there continuously ever since. Was married to Sallie Meloan October 1, 1845. Is the father of 12 children, nine boys and three girls; all except one boy are now living, and all with one exception within an hour's ride of the old homestead. Mr. Wear is the oldest business man in Murray, having been in the drug business on the same lot for more than 43 years, and by a quiet and prudent life is yet able to dose out and dispense quinine and calomel with nearly as much dexterity as his boys, who have nearly all been brought up in the drug trade. In his younger days he took great interest in educational matters, and was one of the originators of Murray Institute, and he with co-laborers spent much time, labor and money is accomplishing the building of that grand institution of learning. He has been identified with many other enterprises of the town since its beginning, in fact, is one of the fathers of the town. Has been successful in business; has never failed to pay all bills in a business life of more than 50 years. He and wife and nearly all of their children and several grand children are members of the Christian church. He is a Royal Arch Mason, and has been the honored Treasurer of that fraternity at Murray for more than 30 years.

A. H. WEAR.

The Town of Benton.

In 1842 the place was selected on a tract of land belonging to Francis Clayton upon which the town of Benton was located, which is now the county seat of Marshall county. It was incorporated by an act of the legislature and approved by his Excellency Wm. Owsley, then governor of the state, January 11, 1845. The charter of the town was first amended September 20, 1861, and a few other similar acts were passed afterwards, and again on March 13, 1878, Governor James B. McCreary approved an act reducing into one all other acts pertaining to the town. All of these acts became null and void by virtue of new laws governing towns of the Sixth class that were passed by the first legislature under the new constitution, and from that time until the present, general, and not special, laws have governed towns of this class.

Barry's Addition was made to the town in 1890, which was made a part of the corporate territory of the town in 1893. The old part of the town was platted and accurately laid off into streets, alleys, etc., by P. Palmer, and ordered to record in the county clerk's office by the county court in May 1874. The town then contained five streets running east and west, and six streets running north and south, and 113 lots and squares. The public square contains 208 feet and eight inches each way.

Benton is situated near the center of the county, about one mile west of Clark's river, and 22 miles south of Paducah, and like the great city of Rome, she sets on seven hills, surrounded on the south and west by poor hills, and on the east and north by the rich and loamy farming lands of Clark's river bottoms.

The Paducah, Tennessee and Alabama railroad was built in 1890, and runs within one-half mile of the court house, which has greatly added to the life and business prosperity of the town, and has also made it the trade center of the county.

The town was named in honor of Thomas H. Benton, the great senator of Missouri, and though a small town, it has been the place where many exciting political scenes have been enacted. Some of the state's greatest men have visited this place and have held large crowds enchanted by their magic and convincing eloquence. It has also been the home of some eminent lawyers and astute politicians.

Until recently it never had over 300 souls within its corporate limits, but now it has a population of 1,000 thrifty and industrious people. Since the building of the railroad old houses have been torn down, and in their places new and better ones have been built. It now contains three churches—Methodist, Baptist and Christian; the Marshall County Seminary is also located in the northwest part of the town; four dry goods stores, two drug stores, five groceries, two restaurants, one hardware store, one hotel, two livery stables, one photograph gallery, two millinery stores, one paint store, two butcher shops, a tobacco warehouse, one barbershop, a planing mill, a carding factory, one printing office, a $6,000 flouring mill, seven lawyers, three ministers, four doctors, two boot and shoe shops, one saloon and one Bank.

The railroad company has just completed a new and elegant depot and other conveniences for the business public. The town will continue to grow and improve until it will be a pleasant little county seat town of 1,500 inhabitants. It is a healthy place, and is well supplied with plenty of fine water. The people are moral, hospitable, law-abiding, and never fail to contribute their share to the maintenance of church, state and society.

JUDGE JOHN J. DUPRIEST

Was born April 20, 1831, in Smith county, Tennessee, (now Trousdale county.) He is a son of John Bunyan and Matilda W. Dupriest, and in 1849 came with his parents to Henry county, near Conyersville, where he completed his education in the Conyersville Academy and remained with his parents until 1857, when he came with them and located near Briensburg, in Marshall county, Ky. When the lives, liberty and property of the Southern people began to be endangered by the encroachments of the Abolition party of the north, he at once enlisted in the Confederate army under Col. Alfred Johnston, at Camp Boone,

(For Sketch see page 88.)

but remained there but a short time, when he was honorably discharged on account of hereditary consumption, and returned home. He continued to live with them and work on the farm until October 1, 1867, when he was married to Mrs. Lucy A. Buford. Two children were born to them, Robert L. and Mary P. After two years' residence in Marshall county, they moved to Livingston county, where they lived on a farm until 1874, when they moved back to Marshall county. He was elected and served three years as constable, after which he was deputy sheriff two years under G. S. Jones. In 1878 he was elected Justice of the Peace in the Briensburg district, was re-elected in 1882, and again in 1886, which gave him 12 years on the fiscal court of the county, and it was during his long service as a magistrate that he gained the appellation of the "Watch-dog of the Treasury." He was always found on the side of the taxpayers, and against extravagant appropriations, and in this way he soon won a warm place in the hearts of his countrymen. In August, 1890, he was elected as an independent democrat to the office of County Judge, over T. F. Harrison, the nominee of the democratic party, by a majority of 28 votes. During his four years on the bench he lost none of his former popularity, and was re-elected, as the nominee of the populist party, over J. M. Bean, the nominee of the democratic party, by a majority of 51 votes, on November 6, 1894. His term of office will expire January 1, 1898. He joined the Methodist church September 8, 1850, of which he has been a devoted member ever since. He joined the Masonic lodge in 1858, at Birmingham, and afterward joined the Chapter at Benton. In politics he is a firm admirer of the principles of the populist party. He, by his hard struggles for honest government, has forced his way to the front rank as a popular county official and a man who has the prosperity and welfare of his people at heart.

H. M. HEATH

Was born in Calloway, (now Marshall) county, Ky., near Briensburg, February 16, 1834. He was raised on a farm and attended the country schools of the then sparsely settled country. He was married to Miss Elizabeth Pace on January 3, 1853; ten  children were born to them, five of whom are now living. He joined the Baptist church in December, 1852, and is yet a member. In April, 1862, he joined company B. 36th Arkansas Infantry, Confederate Army, where he remained until he was honorably discharged at Marshall, Texas, July, 1865. In September, 1865, he returned to Kentucky and located at Birmingham, where he began his trade, that of a mechanic, at which he continued until 1890. At the May election 1866 he was elected Justice of the Peace, was re-elected in 1870, serving two full terms. In December, 1875, he was admitted to the bar as a licensed attorney, having passed a rigid examination by W. G. Bullitt and R. W. Wake. In August, 1890, he was elected county attorney, as an independent democrat, his term of office expiring January 1st, 1895. He was married to Mrs. Emma Cole, November 17, 1892, and two children have been born to them, one of which is now living. He has been a man of good physical constitution, and a strong vigorous mind, and is one of the best all-round stump speakers in the county. As a social gentleman his superior can hardly be found in the county. When he retires from office he will give his time to the practice of his profession among the people of his native county.

JAMES R. LEMON.

James R. Lemon, the subject and writer of this sketch, was the oldest child of J. G. and Demarias A. Lemonds. He was born April 10, 1848, in Guilford county, North Carolina, near where the battle of "Guilford Court House" was fought during the Revolutionary war. He came with his parents, in a two horse wagon, to Marshall county, Kentucky, in 1855. He was raised on a farm and attended the public schools of his neighborhood, which were very poor at that time, until 1870, when he taught a subscripton school at Lebanon church, in Henry county, Tenn. On March 27th, of the same year he entered the Marshall county Seminary, under Prof. A. Pomroy. At the close of the spring term he was employed to teach the public school at Salem, in his home district, at the end of which he re-entered the Seminary, where he remained until in April, 1871. He was then employed as clerk in the general store of Col. T. B. Waller, at Briensburg, where he remained until September, when he was employed, as teacher, in the Oak Valley school. At the end of his school he returned home where he lived until August, 1872, when he began the public school at Briensburg, at the end of which he taught a four months subscription school early in 1873. On March 13, 1873, he was married to Miss Cora A. Wilson, of Benton, and as a result of this union four children were born, three of whom are now living, Clay G. Luna E. and Maude S. They began housekeeping in Briensburg; he taught school until March 1874, when he moved to Benton and entered the drug business in partnership with his father-in-law under the firm name of Lemon & Wilson. In a short time he lost his partner by death and he continued the business in his own name until 1880, when he formed a co-partnership with W. A. Holland in the drug and grocery business. In 1880 he was appointed by Col. Sam Gaines, of Hopkinsville, to take the census of the Benton and Oak Level districts. Early in 1881 he was employed by Patrick & Wilson, wholesale dealers in books and stationery, at Evansville, Ind., as traveling salesman, which position he held for five years. In 1883 Holland & Lemon sold out to Barry & Starks, and on November 17, 1884, he bought Barry's interest and the business was conducted by Starks & Lemon until October 13, 1890, when the senior partner retired from the firm, and the business has been conducted since in the name of J. R. Lemon. His wife died March 20, 1885, and left him with three children. On October 6, 1885, he was married to Miss Lucretia C. Thompson, the youngest daughter of Mrs. Martha Thompson. Two children have been born to them, one of which is now living, and is named Scott Thompson. In March, 1886, he was appointed by Governor J. Proctor Knott on the State Board of Equalization, with headquarters at Frankfort, to fill out the unexpired term of C. C.

Coulter, deceased. In November, 1886, he was elected to the same position from the First Congressional district, over several competitors be 3,000 majority. On May 1, 1890, he became the editor and proprietor of the Benton Tribune, which soon became one of the leading county papers in Western Kentucky. As a newspaper man, was a fair writer and a successful manager. He is still proprietor and publisher. In 1892 he was appointed master commissioner of Marshall county by D. G. Park, judge of the court of common pleas, which position he held until he resigned in 1893. He held the post office at Briensburg in 1873 and at Benton for seven years, under the administrations of Grant and Arthur, and on May 9, 1893, was appointed postmaster under Cleveland's administration, at Benton, which position he now holds. He is a Mason, a Knights of Honor, an Odd Fellow, a democrat, a member of the Christian church, and has been trustee of the Marshall County Seminary for fifteen years. He has lived a life of an energetic hard working business man, and never drank whiskey, chewed tobacco, or gambled, and was always punctual to comply with his contracts.

JAMES M. FISHER

Was born in Marshall county, Kentucky, five miles south of Benton, on February 19, 1856. He was raised on a farm and was of poor parentage. His early education was confined to the common schools of his native county. In his sixteenth year he obtained a certificate to teach school; afterwards he would teach a common school and then attend the Marshall County Seminary. This he continued until he obtained a fair English education. In the year 1876 he began the study of law under Hon. W. M. Reed, of Benton, Ky., giving to the study what spare time he had from teaching and farm work. In June 1877, he obtained a license to practice law and after being examined by Hon. W. G. Bullitt, of Paducah, and Hon. R. W. Wake, of Eddyville, and after being admitted to the bar he was compelled to teach school and farm for a livelihood until 1880. He was married October 17, 1878, to Miss Ida Ely, a daughter of Jack Ely, deceased; by this union they had born to them seven children, four of whom are still living, After his marriage he lived on a farm, two miles west of Benton, until February, 1880, when he moved to Benton and began the practice of law, and in June following formed a co-partnership with Hon. W L. Weathers, of Murray, Ky which continued until the death of Mr. Weathers. In the following July he was elected, by the magistrates of Marshall county, School Commissioner, which office he held one term. In August, 1882, he was elected County Attorney for Marshall county, over J. W. Holland, of Birmingham, Ky., and after serving one term was re-elected in 1886. In the discharge of the trusts confided to him, by his people, either in a public office or as an individual, he has always proven himself to be honest, competent and able. Notwithstanding the public trusts that had been confided to him and the duties incumbent upon him as a public officer, he has, by his energy and industry (two very prominent characteristics of his life) built up for himself a very fair practice in his profession. On December 2, 1889, his wife died. In June, 1890, he formed a partnership in the practice of law with Hon. J. W. Dycus, of Benton, and continued said partnership until May, 1892, when said partnership was dissolved by mutual consent, and he formed a partnership with J. M. Bean, esq., and continued with him until February, 1894, when said partnership was dissolved. Since which time he has been practicing his profession alone. In 1892 he made the race for the democratic nomination for Commonwealth's Attorney for the Second Judicial district of Kentucky, against W. F. Bradshaw and Oscar Kahn, of Paducah, and was defeated by Hon. W. F. Bradshaw. He is an uncompromising democrat

JAS. M. FISHER.

and has been all his life. He is a member of the Christian church, and has been since 1891; he is also a member of the Independent Order of Odd Fellows with the title of Past Grand. He is regarded one of the best lawyers in Western Kentucky.

JOHN G. LOVETT.

The subject of this sketch, was born on a farm, in the southeast portion of Marshall county, Kentucky, May the 9th, 1869. He is the son of John and Elizabeth Lovett, deceased; his parents were very poor and unable to send him to school; his early education was therefore neglected. His parents both died when John was eighteen years of age; leaving him without a dollar, and he could not then write his name, but he desired to abtain an education, and through the assistance of his elder brother D. A. Lovett, he borrowed money enough to go to school one year, and at once entered Wadesboro school, under the tutorship of J. K. Wells; and at the end of this session he had made such rapid progress he obtained a certificate to teach and commenced teaching the common schools of the county, and continued teaching during the fall months, and going to school during the spring and summer, until he got out of debt and saved enough money to go to college; and on January 1, 1889, he entered the State College of Lexington, Ky., where he completed his education. While there he joined a debating society in which he took great interest, and established a reputation of being a witty debator and brilliant orator. After returning from Lexington he taught one more very successful school, and January 1, 1890, he entered the law office of Judge Dycus as a student, for he was determined from the start (notwithstanding having to battle all the time against poverty) to become a lawyer, he devoted himself to close study and on June 12, 1890, he was admitted to the Bar of Benton, after passing a most rigid but satisfactory examination. After being admitted to the bar he taught school two years, during which time he continued his law studies. On February 24, 1892, he was married to Miss Laura Frizzell; a very beautiful and accomplished young lady, of Birmingham. One child has blessed this union, Lala, a very intelligent little girl, born August 31, 1893. In June, 1892, Mr Lovett retired from teaching and moved to Benton and adopted law as his profession, and has been actively engaged in the same ever since. But few young lawyers enjoy as good a practice as John; he ranks among the best young lawyers of Western Kentucky. He is not a member of any church, but is sober and moral. In politics he is an uncompromising democrat. On March 10, 1894, he was nominated by the democratic party for County Attorney and from then until the November election he made an active and heated campaign. His opponent was Mr. H. M. Heath, who was a candidate for re-election, but Mr. Lovett defeated him on the 6th of November, 1894, by the overwhelming majority of 1,116 votes, carrying every precinct in the county. He will take charge of his office the 1st of January, 1895, and will make one of the best attorneys the county has ever had. He is greatly devoted to his family, is of a cheerful and social disposition and is true to his friends and kind to his enemies. Is 28 years of age, a close student, able prosecutor and a magnetic speaker, and has a bright future. Is a noble example of a self-made man, born and raised in poverty, with patient toil and a laudable ambition in early years, he has laid the foundation for fame and success.

CLAY GALDSTONE LEMON

Was born July 9, 1876, in the town of Benton, Marshall county

Kentucky. He is the oldest son of J. R. and Cora A. Lemon. His mother died March 20, 1885. He entered school at the Marshall County Seminary when six years old and continued until February 10, 1887, when he was elected Page of the State Board of Equalization at Frankfort, Ky., which place he filled for two years. He returned home and continued in school until July 1, 1893, when he was appointed Assistant Postmaster, under his father, at Benton, which position he now holds. He is sober, moral, attentive to business and has bright prospects before him as a business young man.

LOUIS E. WALLACE

Present School Superintendent was born in Monroe county, Illinois, April 25, 1858. He is the oldest son of Elder I. E. and Mrs. Sarah Wallace. His mother died in 1864 and in the same year he came with his father to Marshall county, Kentucky and located in the western part of the county. He worked on the farm and attended the public schools of his neighborhood until he was twenty years old, when he attended a private school taught by J. M. Quinn at Symsonia, Graves county. In 1879 he began teaching the public schools and continued in the work until he had taught 59 months, partly in Graves and partly in Marshall county. He received the democratic nomination and was elected County School Superintendent in 1890, and was re-elected in November, 1893. His present term of office will expire January 1, 1898. He was married May 5, 1885, to Miss A. M. Riley. Two children, Guy and Ina, have been born to them. He is not a member of any church or secret society, but is a true democrat. He is making the county an excellent superintendent, giving his entire time and attention to the duties of the office.

SOLON L. PALMER

Was born in Benton, Marshall county, Kentucky., February 8, 1865, and is the youngest son of Philander and Susan A. Palmer. He was raised in town and educated in the Marshall County Seminary. He was appointed deputy sheriff, under W. W. English, at the age of seventeen, which position he held for three years. In August, 1886, he was elected Circuit Court Clerk of Marshall county, when he was just past twenty-one years old, which position he held for a full term of six years. He was appointed Master Commissioner by C. L. Randle, judge of the Marshall Circuit Court in December, 1886, and made one of the most acceptable commissioners that ever held that position in the county. The attention he gave, and the ability developed, in performing the duties of clerk and commissioner, won for him the reputation of a sober, safe and capable business young man. In 1890 when the stock was subscribed, and the Bank of Benton was organized, the attention of the directors pointed to young Palmer as the most suitable person to perform the responsible and important duties of cashier. He was elected to that position, which he now holds, and it has been under his care and business management that the new bank has grown and prospered until it is now one of the safest and best managed financial institutions in this end of the State. He is fast pushing his way to the front rank as an able and wise financier, and not many years will pass before his services will be in ready demand in the largest banking institutions of the country. He was married June 9, 1886, to Miss Clemmie Coleman an accomplished young lady, of Murray, Ky., at Brownsville, Tenn. He joined the Methodist church in 1878, and for the past thirteen years has been the popular superintendent of the Sunday school at his church. He is an Odd Fellow, a Knight of Honor and a democrat.

JUDGE JAMES V. WEAR,

Seventh son of Archibald H. and Sallie Wear, was born in Murray, Calloway county, Ky., June 13, 1865. Was raised on a farm where he remained until he was 18 years of age, when

JUDGE JAS. V. WEAR.

he went to Fulton, Ky., and remained one year and a half in the drug business with his brother, Wm. O. Wear. Returned to Murray, in October, 1884, and engaged in the printing business until August, 1887, when he went to Paris, Tennessee, and there engaged in the same business, where he remained for one year. From September, 1888 till August, 1889, he was engaged in the printing trade at Princeton, Kentucky. On August 1, 1889, he formed the Wear Printing Company, at Murray, and purchased the Murray Weekly News, which paper he managed until December 30, 1890, when he sold his interest in said Company and moved to Paducah, Ky. There he established the Purchase Journal, and later he was interested in the publication of the Saturday Journal and the Sunday

Truth, where he continued until December, 1891. On December 30, 1891, he was married to Miss Edna E. Marshall, the oldest daughter of C. C. Marshall, of Murray, Ky. He and his wife have been blessed with two children, Estelle and Annie B., two bright little girls. On January 1, 1892, he moved to Benton to take charge of the mechanical department of the Benton Tribune, which place he still occupies. Having been identified as a citizen of Benton, on November 7, 1893, he was elected Police Judge of the town of Benton, over T. H. Blewett, the then Judge, by a good majority. He entered upon his duties as such Judge, in January 1894, and by his judicial firmness, in dealing with the violaters of the law, has won for himself the respect and friendship of all classes. He has identified himself with the people of Marshall county in a way that has made him a prominent citizen of the county.

W. R. FIELDS

Was born near Briensburg, Marshall county, Ky., January 13, 1859. He is a son of John W. and Nancy E. Fields. He was raised and educated on the farm, attended only the best of the common schools of his community. By close study he received a good business English education. He was married September 27, 1878, to Miss Samantha A. Wyatt; eight children blessed this union, seven of which are now living. He continued to labor on the farm until he was 21 years old, soon after which he was elected constable in his district, and served one term of two years. He joined the Christian church at "Old Union," in 1874 under the preaching of Elder J. F. McCoy, but was baptized by Elder James Lindsey. In 1888 he moved to Sharpe, where he at present resides. Since he located there he has had the business management of the Oakland Patent Roller Mills, that are now owned by Capt. J. M. Watson. He has given his entire time and attention to the business, in fact he is regarded the best superintendent of a patent roller mill in the county. He belongs to no secret society, and in politics is a democrat. He has always been a moral, sober, live, energetic business man and is classed among the county's most influential citizens.

The Town of Birmingham.

The town of Birmingham is situated twelve miles east of Benton, on Tennessee river, and was located in 1849 on a tract of land belonging to Thomas A. Grubbs, and was laid out and platted as a town in 1853, and was incorporated by an act of the Legislature February 27, 1860. Love's Addition was added to it, and became a part of the town in 1858. L. S. Locker and Thomas Love arrived and became the first settlers September 12, 1849, but when they first came there was one house and an old shed in the town. When they landed on this side of the river James L. Brown, now living in Paducah, was there with an ox team, and then hauled the first wagon load of goods up the bank into what is now the town of Birmingham that was ever hauled in that place.

Among the early settlers were John H. Hamilton and John Frizzell, and a little later on, in 1851, Thomas A. Grubbs came; in 1856 James Love, the biggest tobacco man in the Purchase, located there, and in 1857 John Lockhead arrived and ran a grist mill for three years, after which he began merchandising, and so continued until the time of his death.

The town continued to prosper until 1866. Depue and C. M. Brown located their stave manufactory there, and at one time this firm employed from 125 to 150 hands in the stave and timber business. The town was at its best at that time, and in all probability will never do so much business again. In 1867 it contained 476 inhabitants; in 1870, 322; in 1880, 224; in 1890, 201, which shows the damaging effects the building of railroads had upon its commerce. It has three churches, a Methodist Episcopal, a Methodist Church South and a Missionary Baptist. There are also two colored churches, one a Methodist, the other a Baptist. Two schools, one white, one colored, two hotels, four dry-goods and general stores, three groceries, one drug store, two millinery stores, two wagon and blacksmith shops, two ministers of the gospel, one physician, two dentists, one speculator and several contractors and mechanics. City officers are T. A. Travis, City Judge; J. J. Hendrick, City Marshal; W. S. Stone, J. T. Barnett, J. E. Long and J. N. Goheen councilmen. W. M. Holland is the present postmaster, a democrat appointed under Mr. Cleveland's administration.

The town is situated above high water mark, and is surrounded by a rich section of farming lands. The people are industrious, moral and upright, and have all that sociability and hospitality for which Kentuckians are noted. Before the building of railroads this town was the shipping point for all the surrounding country. The first store house ever built in the town was built of hickory logs in 1849, and it is still standing, and is used by L. S. Locker for a warehouse.

Ab Smith and Lucas Holland sawed the corners off the first log house that was ever built in the town.

Locker & Hall was the style of a firm doing business in Birmingham 45 years ago.

Hastin Smith was born in North Carolina and came from what is now Calloway county, Ky., in 1829, and settled within three miles of the town, and lived on the same farm from that time until 1855, when he died. He raised four children, two boys and two girls.

Ab Smith, a son of Hastin Smith, came with his parents from Calloway county when he was 18 months old, and has lived 52 years in the same magisterial district, during which he was six years constable, two years Police Judge of Birmingham, and eight years a justice of the peace. Is a Methodist and a populist.

EDWARD ZUECKLER

Is a native of Saxony, and was born 1839 in the city of Zwickau

of that State. His parents were well-to-do people, and his father a noted pharmacist. After receiving a liberal education, both in German and Latin schools, he went to Italy, where he spent five years as correspondent clerk for a prominent commission merchant of Venice. In 1861 he emigrated to the United States, where, after occupying several positions as book-keeper in Philadelphia, he engaged in the oil business in the western part of the state of Pennsylvania. At first he was successful and rapidly accumulated much money but lost it all in the great crash of 1875. Despairing of ever mending his broken fortunes went south and after years of hard labor, finally located in Marshall county, Kentucky, where he is well known as a successful fruit tree agent and prospector for iron ore and native minerals. Through the death of his parents he came into possession of a moderate fortune some of which he invested in fine farming lands in the county and a part in the drug business at Birmingham of which business he has made a success and is highly appreciated as an honest and capable business man. He is unmarried and a democratic voter.

MISS META LOVE

Was born in Birmingham, Marshall county, Kentucky. She is the daughter of Mr. and Mrs. James Love, of that town. She

was educated in the best schools of her town besides she finished her business education in Evansville, Ind., and also took music which she kept up; and while in school was the same modest, obedient child that she is now a woman, and her pleasant manners and happy disposition won for her the lasting friendship of all of her acquaintances and associates. She is a member of the M. E. church, and in 1891 began to rely upon her own labor for a living by engaging in the millinery business in her native town, and among her friends and neighbors. She studied the business and worked early and late, in order to please her customers, and master the situation. This she has done, as is evidenced by the thriving business she has built up and the success that has attended her efforts. Her ambition is laudable, and her energy is being daily rewarded by hard and honest evil.

OSCAR T. GREGORY,

One of the county's prominent business young men, was born may 8, 1872, near the residence of W. C. Holland, nine miles east of Benton. He is the oldest child of Marion and Laura (nee Goheen) Gregory. Attended the common schools of his neighborhood only six months. His father died when he was eleven years old; worked on the farm until he was 18 years old, since which time he has been selling territory for patent rights, principally for the C. E. Cardwell Automatic Latching Gate. He is now owner of the territory of the United States and is doing business at present in many states disposing of unsold territory. He is reckoned one of the most successful patent right salesmen in the country. He has grown nearly rich at the business and is the owner of valuable property in several states. He is unmarried, belongs to no church or secret society, is honest and sober and in politics is a democrat.

HENRY HOLLAND

Was born March 2, 1871, near Birmingham, Marshall county, Kentucky. His parents, J. L. and M. A. Holland, are natives of Kentucky. He was raised on a farm and until he was nearly grown attended the common school of his home district. In the spring of 1891, he left the farm and spent some time flat-boating on Tennessee, Ohio and Missippi rivers, and during the entire time he never drank whisky, played cards or swore an oath. He soon began to feel the need of an education and returned home and entered school under J. G.

Lovett. In 1892 he taught school, after which he attended two sessions at the Murray Institute, and after he came home was employed as teacher in district No. 36 where he is now teaching with a first class certificate. He is a young man of good address, a member of the Oriental Order of Humility, and an organization democrat. He is one of the coming young men of his day.

LABAN SHIPPS LOCKER

Was born September 14, 1819, in Hopkinsville, Christian county Kentucky. When fifteen years old he was sent to Lexington, Kentucky, where he remained seven months in the postoffice under a very staunch old democrat, Joseph Fickline, then postmaster, after which he returned home and worked about in stores for over two years. In 1837 he moved to Eddyville, where he did business for A. B. Kinkead and assisted his employer to move to Paducah, in December 1837, when it was a very small town. He was engaged to do business at Eddyville for Cobbs, Gray & Bell, then the principal merchants of the place. Remained with them until the close of 1840, when he was married to Miss Judith L. Goodall. They lived in Caldwell county until 1849, when they came, with Thomas Love, to the place where Birmingham now stands. He and Thos. Love dug the first well, and built the first school house, which house was always used for the circuit rider and others that came to preach to them. The first sermon ever preached in the place was preached by Elder James Lindsey; it was preached in Love's old tobacco factory. He looks back to the old times when Lindsey, Levi Lee and other used to preach; these were perhaps the happiest days of all. He says in those times he could buy a fine fat turkey for a bar of lead, and that wild meat was in abundance and sold at very low prices. All of the country about Briensburg, Palma, Calvert City, Gilbertsville and Olive were then tributary to Birmingham, and the people came to buy provisions, etc. Mr. Locker is familiar with everything in detail that has occurred in and about Birmingham since his arrival there in 1849.

Briensburg, Kentucky.

The village of Briensburg was named in honor of James Brien, and was incorporated February 18, 1861. The plat of the town was made by J. G. Haydock, who now resides in Bloomfield, Mo., and who was then county surveyor; it consists of 17 blocks and other territory not laid off. The town is located near the center of the county, on the level highlands, between Tennessee and Clark's rivers, and is surrounded by a section of country thickly settled with industrious, law-abiding christian people. It has about 200 inhabitants, three general stores, one millinery store, two blacksmith and wagon shops, two churches, one a Methodist, other a Christian, one good school house, one masonic lodge, three physicians and two ministers.

In 1880 it had a population of 67, but has more than doubled in the past ten years. It is not making much improvements, yet it is more than holding its own in business and general prosperity.

W. W. Nimmo was appointed postmaster under Mr. Cleveland in 1894, which position he will hold until there is a change in the politics of the administration.

This town was always a candidate for the county seat, and for many years there were two county seat factions, one for it to remain at Benton, and the other for it to be moved, either to Briensburg or Birmingham, but when the railroad was built through the county via Benton, this ended the old county seat fight, which was a disturbing question for over a generation.

Briensburg has been the home of several prominent families, among them the Lackey's, Locker's, Burradell's, Holland's, Graham's, Cook's, Thomas', Brien's, Mooney's, Walker's, Waller's, Fields', Nimmo's, Wyatt's, and a long list of other worthies whose names are almost forgotten and effaced from the memories of those now living.

Many happy memories will ever cluster about the little village of Briensburg in the mind of the writer of this little book, for it was in it he laid the foundation for his business life.

L. J. GOSSETT.

L. J. GOSSETT.

The subject of this sketch was born in Muhlenburg county, Kentucky, July 25, 1860. Isaac Gossett, his father, was a native of Kentucky, and his mother, Susan Gossett, was born in North Carolina, but their son was raised on a farm and was educated in the common schools until 1878, when he entered West Kentucky Classical Normal College, where he remained for about three years. He taught three public schools after which he came to Marshall county and began the general merchandise business at Briensburg. Was married to Miss Lizzie Fields September 29, 1887. She died of consumption May 20, 1892. He was married the second time to Mrs. Alice Felds March 29, 1893. In politics he is a prohibitionist, and has been a member of the Christian church since 1877. He is a member of the city council, superintendent of the Sunday School and vice president of the Sunday School union. His wife, Mrs. Alice Gossett, was born July 7, 1859, raised and educated in Marshall county, was married to J. Louis Fields in 1879, whose death took place November 21, 1884. She lived a widow until March 29, 1893. She has been a member of the Christian church since 1873, and has always lived the life of a christian woman and is highly esteemed by all who know her.

The Town of Hardin.

The new town of Hardin was located by R. W. Starks and John T. Irvan, partly on a tract of land owned by H. D. Irvan & Sons and partly on a tract of land owned by R. W. Starks, of Hardin, and J. R. Smith, of Paducah. It was begun June 5, 1891, by laying off three streets running north and south and four streets running east and west, containing nine blocks and 132 lots, with plenty of other lands adjacent thereto. The town was run out and the plat made by J. W. Stewart, of Calloway county, and recorded in the Clerk's office at Benton in deed book 17, and on pages 570--571. It is situated on the east side of the Paducah, Tennessee and Alabama railroad, eight miles south of Benton, the county seat, two miles east of old Wadesboro, two and one-half miles west of Clark's river, and on the old dirt road leading from Canton to Columbus, Ky. It has two churches, one a Methodist, the other a Missionary Baptist; one good school house worth $1,000, five dry-goods and general stores, four groceries, one hardware store; one hotel one boarding house, one blacksmith shop, one livery stable, one shoe shop, one barber shop, one rehandling tobacco warehouse, two saw mills, one photograph gallery, two physicians, one new passenger depot just completed, and several contractors and mechanics. It is situated in one of the best farming sections of the county, surrounded by a sober, moral, law-abiding, prosperous people. Though the town is but little over three years old, yet it is the second best town in the county, with a population of 254, and if it continues to prosper in the future, as it has done in the past, it will soon be a thriving little city of 500 inhabitants. It derived its name from the given name of "Hardin" Irvan, and hence the name Hardin.

John T. Irvan is the polite postmaster, under the present administration, and he is also the agent for the railroad company.

The town has never been incorporated under the laws of the State, and unless there is a change in the sentiment of its leading citizens, in this respect, it will not be for several years yet to come. The location is healthy, the town well watered and surrounded by everything necessary to make Hardin a town of some commercial importance.

R. W. STARKS,

Of Hardin, Ky., was born March 3, 1848, in the south part of the county. His parents, Spencer P. and Mary Starks, are some of the pioneers of the county. He was educated in the common schools of his neighborhood and was raised on a farm. He was married on February 29, 1871, to Miss Rebecca F. Hurt, by Elder N. Darnall, and three children are the result of this union, L. C., N. P., and O. P. Starks. He began a general merchandise business at Olive in 1880, and remained there until April, 1892, when he erected a new brick store house at Hardin and became a citizen of that place, where he is now doing a large mercantile business. He was elected magistrate in 1876, and after serving nearly 12 years as one of the county's best guardians, he resigned and moved to Hardin. Was postmaster at Olive about 8 years. He was baptised into the Christian church 28 years ago by Elder J. F. McCoy. He is a Mason, an Odd Fellow, and a member of the Oriental Order of Humility. There is no better citizen in the county than R. W. Starks.

R. W. STARKS.

ROBERT CLINTON BOYD.

Robert Clinton Boyd, whose picture appears in this sketch, was born June 18, 1858, in Weakly county, Tennessee. He is the youngest son of J. M. Boyd, of Olive, Kentucky. His mother was Artely Paschal. His father moved to this state and county when "Bob" was but 6 years old. He settled on the Boaz Williams place, one mile north of Olive, where he still resides. "Bob" worked on the farm in summer and attended the free schools at Olive in winter, where he always stood well in his classes, both as to deportment and scholarship. Besides the free schools he attended twelve months graded schools, under "Tim" Stamps, at Hico, and John W. Holsapple, at Olive. At the age of 18 he was examined for a teacher's certificate receiving the highest average per cent of anyone on that day. For five years he taught school in the county, ranking among the best teachers of the county. He taught 24 months in all. At 23 he married

Miss Anna Gregory, of Fair Dealing, who by her gentleness, kindness, charity, religion sociability and multiplicity of good graces has done much to smooth the rough places, lighten the burdens and let sunshine into the otherwise grum character of her liege lord. For 8 years he lived on the Dave Gardner farm, one mile west of Olive, following farming with moderate success; but seeing that the farm was not the place for him, he left it and traveled for two years for the Wrought Iron Range company, of St Louis. He proved a blooming success as a traveling salesman, making money both for himself and his company. Traveling not being altogether satisfactory, and realizing that if he could make money for others he could do so for himself, he located in 1891 at the new town of Hardin where he conducts a grocery, hardware and furniture store, second to none in the county and is enjoying a large and remunerative trade. In politics Mr. Boyd is a democrat and in religion a Baptist. Mr. Boyd is a man of strong intellectuality and physically a perfect man. No one enjoys life more or is more happily situated in business. He is one of the county's best citizens, and such men as he is, and happy families as his, contribute largely to the prosperity of the country and the building up of society.

DR. THOMAS EMMET RUSSELL,

The subject of this sketch, was born in Calloway county, Ky., August 20, 1860. He was the youngest son of John G. Russell. He attended the free school at Temple Hill and the High School at Murray. He began the study of medicine, when quite young, under Dr. J. T. Gingles, it being the natural bend of his mind; he entered the Medical University of Louisville, Ky., in 1883, and graduated in 1886, with the highest honors of his class. He located at Olive, Ky., where he soon built up a profitable practice In 1885 his father becoming ill he returned to Calloway county where he remained until the new

DR. T. E. RUSSELL.

town of Hardin sprang up, where he located, and is now a useful and prominent citizen, having a large and remunerative practice. In his profession he is methodical, painstaking and successful. In 1892-93 the professionable ability that he displayed in treating that much dreaded disease, "spotted fever," added new laurels to his fame and rapidly won for him a name that will live long after he is gone. In 1893 he was married to Miss Ellie Faircloth, an accomplished and refined young lady from the famous Bluegrass Region of Kentucky. In politics Dr. Russell is a "simon pure" democrat, and a member of the Cumberland Presbyterian church. His name will ever remain sacred in the memory of all who know him for his many acts of kindness.

DR. W. PUCKETT

Was born in Calloway county, Ky., March 10, 1850, but was raised on a farm in Marshall county. His educational advantages were very poor, yet he attended the public schools of his community and by close study and hard work gained a common English education, which has greatly assisted him in after years. He had an ambition to become learned in medicine, and in due time began its study under Dr. W. H. Clark, of this county, and continued it until now he is doing a good practice in the southeast part of the county. He has been married twice, his first wife was Miss Fannie Tyree and his present wife was Miss S. C. Groves. Doctor Puckett is a social, clever gentleman and stands well among his neighbors as a useful citizen.

Calvert City.

The town of Calvert City is one of the best towns in the county. It is situated in the north part of the county on the Chesapeake Ohio and Southwestern railroad and was incorporated March 18, 1871, and laid off and platted into a town in 1872 with nineteen blocks and 133 lots, six streets east and six west, each sixty feet wide. It has a population of 200, and is situated in a fine farming section of the county.

It has a depot, a hotel, one mill, two churches—one a Missionary Baptist, the other a Union church, occupied jointly between the Methodist and Christian brethren; two general stores, on drug store, one blacksmith shop, two physicians and several mechanics. W. A. Freeman is the democratic postmaster. It is a good business point, where the farmers come from the surrounding country to do their trading.

It was named in honor of P. W. Calvert, who is still living within its corporate limits, and is one of its most enterprising and useful citizens.

DR. L. E. FINLEY

Was born in Trigg county, Kentucky, March 21, 1852; was

raised on the farm and received only a common school education in the public schools of his home district. He came to Marshall county when he was quite young and settled in the northeast part of the county in the vicinity of Calvert City. He was married October 22, 1873 to Miss Willie P. Miller and several children have blessed their union, the ceremony was performed by Eld. T. F. Harrison. In 1882 he began the study of medicine under Dr. E. P. Rucker, soon after which he attended a course of lectures in the medical school of Memphis, Tenn.

He returned home and studiously continued his studies until June 20, 1890, when he graduated with honors from the Kentucky School of Medicine, Louisville, Ky. He came home and located at Calvert City, where he has since enjoyed an excellent practice. He is regarded as a very successful physician and is called far and near in consultation with the most reputable practioners in the county. He is a man of great energy and never shirks his duty. He is social and clever and never forsakes a friend in trouble. He has an interesting family. In religion he is a Baptist, in politics a republican. He is one of the county's most conspicuous characters.

W. W. ENGLISH

Was born in Livingston county, Ky., near Gum Spring church, on May 25, 1854; moved with his parents to Marshall county in 1864. He was raised on the farm, but received a very good English education, considering the grade of schools he attended. At 18 years of age he spent a short time teaching, but at the age of 22, which was in 1876, he was elected constable, and in 1878 he was re-elected, and served in that position until 1880, when he was elected to the office of high sheriff in 1882; he was re-elected to the same position without opposition; he was appointed, by Judge Campbell, master commissioner, which position he held for three years. After his term of office expired he returned to his farm where he has been engaged in farming and in the saw mill business most of the time since. He was married to Miss Elizabeth

Harper, daughter of Wm Harper, March 5, 1873. Five children have blessed this union, three of which are now living, Thos. W., Ruth A. and Maude M. In March 1894 he was admitted to the bar as a licensed lawyer, in which profession he is now engaged.

DR. R. M. JONES

Was born near Owingsville, Bath county, Ky., November 6th, 1857. His parents died when he was 13 years old. He would work on a farm and attend school until he graduated at the University of Indiana in 1881, after which he was professor of mathematics in the West Kentucky Normal School. He was the principal of the High school at Saramento, Ky., for several years, during which time he distinguished himself as an educator of marked ability. It was during the time he was engaged in teaching that he began the study of medicine; and gave it close attention until June 28, 1889, when he graduated at the Kentucky school of Medicine, Louisville, Ky. He returned from college and practiced his profession at St. Charles, Hopkins county, Ky., for a while, after which he came to Marshall county and located at Calvert City, where he has since given his time to his profession, and now enjoys a fine practice. He was married October 18, 1883, to Miss Lillie Joyce, of Muhlenburg county; two children have blessed this union, a daughter and son, aged respectfully eight and five years. He is the fourth son of a family who were French Exiles. They were among the first, to join the Christian church under the preaching of Alexander Campbell. He has two brothers, who are ministers in that church, S. S. Jones, of Danville, Ill., and Silas Jones, of Cambridge, Mass. He is a member of the U. S. Examining Board of Pensions at Kuttawa, Ky., and local surgeon for the C., O. & S. W. railroad company. He is a member of the Christian church, a Mason and a sound democrat.

A Zealous Worker for the Lord.

ELD. D. M. GREEN.

The name that heads this biography is one of the pioneer preachers of this country. He was born on Piney Creek, Crittenden, county, Kentucky, November 30, 1819. He was raised on a farm, with no educational advantages whatever, but he was a handsome boy with plenty of energy, fine address and strong native ability. He was raised in the faith of the Cumberland Presbyterians, and he began speaking in public when at the age of 17, but never joined the Baptist church until 1850. In 1853 he came to Marshall county to assist in organizing a church. He married Miss E. G. Love in 1839, and eight children were the fruits of this union. He was married the second time in 1861, to Miss Martha E. Roberts and nine children blessed this union, making a total number of 17 children, seven of whom are dead and seven married. He has 29 grand children and seven great grand children. He has lived in two states, six counties and in fourteen neighborhoods. He has done much preaching and has baptized in the Mississippi, Ohio, Cumberland, Tennessee and in many smaller rivers, lakes and ponds in both heat and cold. He has labored with many old veteran preachers that have long since crossed the river to their reward, among some of them are James Mansfield, Collin Hodge, Willis Champion, Ephram Owens, Wm., Sam and Lowery McClain, Robt. Williams and many others. Elder Green is yet living and is as active and energetic as most men of half his age. He has been a faithful stalwart minister in the Baptist church, and has worked all his long life for the good of souls and society.

Gilbertsville.

This village consists of two stores and several residences. it was laid out as a town in 1874, and named in honor of Hon. J. C. Gilbert. It is located at the intersection of the Chesapeake, Ohio and Southwestern railroad and Tennessee river. It is surrounded by one of the best sections of farming lands in the county, and will always be a good trading point.

BEN HOUSTON.

Ben Houston was born in Muhlenburg county, Kentucky, June 14, 1842. He was raised on a farm and received a limited education in such schools as were convenient to him when a boy. At the age of 19 he professed religion and joined the Freewill Baptist, but in 1881 he left that church and joined the Missionary Baptist, of which he has lived a consistent member ever since. In September, 1862, he volunteered and joined the Confederate army, division of cavalry, under General John H. Morgan, serving as a brave and gallant soldier until the close of the war. He resided awhile in West Tennessee, after which he moved to Marshall county and located near Gilbertsville, where he is now engaged in farming. He was elected Justice of the Peace in 1890 and his term of office will expire January 1, 1895. He has made one of the best and safest men on the bench of the fiscal court and is one of the county's best citizens.

ATTIE HOUSTON,

Whose parents are Mr. and Mrs. Ben Houston, of this county, is a true daughter of Kentucky, having a long ancestral descent extending back to the early settlement of this state. Her grand parents on the mother's side, being Mr. and Mrs. Ben Whittaker, whose home is near Green River in McLean county, and on the father's side Mr. and Mrs. William Houston, whose home was also in the same county. Eleven children have been born unto Mr. and Mrs. Ben Houston, viz: Estella, Attie, Sam, Maggie, Lena, Willie, Crow, Flora, May, Boyd and Nellie. Attie being the second child. She was born November 20, 1868, in McLean county, Ky. While very young she moved with her parents to Gibson county, Tenn., where she received the principal part of her education, and entered upon her career as teacher. This

ATTIE HOUSTON

being her favorite calling, she was successful from the first. Books were ever her favorite companions. Her father having a large family to support, five of whom are girls, could not give her educational advantages she desired, but her thirst for knowledge, combined with her indomitable will, enabled her to overcome all obstacles, surmount every difficulty and to go "Onward and upward." Her general disposition is bright, cheerful and social, while her mind is deeply imbued with religious sentiments. She became a member of the Baptist church at the age of 13, and since then has lived a consistent member. She returned to her native state with her father's family in 1889, since which time she has been actively engaged in school work. She holds a first class certificate and has taught 52 months in Marshall county, Ky. She is now teaching in District No. 52. She is single, and by her profession supports herself and helps in educating her younger brothers and sisters.

Some of Our Popular Educators.

PROF. T. D. BROWN

Was born in the southeast part of Marshall county, Kentucky, March 1, 1851. He was the only son of David and Mahala Brown. His mother died when he was nine years old and he was left as a poor boy with no advantages, whatever. He was raised on the farm as a hired hand, working here and there until he was 16 years old, when he began life for himself. Previous to this time he only attended school seven months. He now decided in his mind that he would educate himself, regardless of his poverty. He began to work a while, and go to school the rest of his time, and in this way by close economy and hard study was qualified to begin teaching at the age of eighteen, and for five years would teach and work, and pursue his studies. In 1874 he entered the Marshall County Seminary, where he attended a few sessions, and in June, 1876, was married to Miss Sarah Jane Lee. Eight children have been born to them, seven of whom are now living. In 1874 he was awarded a first-class certificate, and has never been without one since. He was one of the county examiners for six years. Is a member of the Christian church, and also of the alliance and in politics a populist. Prof. Brown is one of the most popular teachers in the county, and has given more of his time to that profession than probably any man of his age in the state. Though he is now comparatively a young man, yet he has taught 186 months, up to the present time. This is a monument to a boy of his opportunities.

WILLIAM BARNHART,

A son of Joshua and Mariah Barnhart, was born July 4, 1847. Was raised on a farm and educated in the common schools of this and adjoining counties. Attended Blandville College five months, and then persued his studies and worked on a farm until 1866, when he taught his first school is district 48 in Marshall county, the same place he is now teaching. He was married to Miss Jennie, daughter of M. B. and A. A. Grace, October 26, 1873, the marriage ceremony being performed by the Rev. E. W. Benson. In 1876–7 he clerked for Wm. Penn & Co; in 1878 for C. Hanna, and also for Stratton & Bird, wholesale grocers, Cairo, Ills.

Then he worked awhile for Rosenbaum & Schwab, at Paducah, Ky. In 1883 he made the race for a seat in the Legislature from the counties of Marshall and Lyon; he also made an unsuccessful race for delegate to the constitutional convention from Calloway county. He is a member of the M. E. Church South. Was appointed by Gov. Brown as the first Police Judge of Dexter, which position he yet holds. He has lived an active life, and is a man of fine information. Notwithstanding he has not given all of his time to teaching, yet he has taught 72 months, in which he has given good satisfaction as a teacher. He lives at Dexter, Calloway county.

GEORGE W. OLIVER,

One of the best young teachers in the county, was born seven miles north of Benton, Marshall county, Ky., August 2, 1869. He is a son of J. N. and Mary E. Oliver. He would work on the farm in the summer and attend the public schools in the fall until he was seventeen years old, when he went to Church Grove and began school under the able instruction of Prof. T. D. Brown, where he remained a full term, after which he attended the Marshall County Seminary for a time. At the age of twenty-one he began the study of law under his brother, W. M. Oliver, and

continued it until June 14, 1891, when, after an examination, by J. M. Fisher and W. M. Reed, a license to practice law was granted him, but so far has never given his entire time to the practice of the profession. For three years he has devoted his time to law, insurance and teaching, and is now engaged in a successful school in district No. 51. On March 10, 1894, he was defeated by a small majority for the democratic nomination for county clerk. He joined the Christian church in August, 1893; has never married or joined any secret society, but in politics is a simon-pure democrat. He is possessed with a strong physical constitution, a vigorous mind and an energy sufficient to make him a man of power and influence among his people.

CLAUDE H. HAMILTON,

The oldest son of W. B. and Sarah M. Hamilton, was born on

January 7, 1871, near Fair Dealing, Marshall county. When about six years old his parents moved with him to Briensburg, where he spent over 15 years of his life, and there secured a good English education. Holds a first-class certificate, has been teaching four years, and is now at Sharpe, where he has a successful school. Taught three terms in Stahl's district, and gives good satisfaction wherever he goes. Has been a member of the Methodist church since November, 1885, and is known for his strict integrity, high morals and good business qualities. Was married May 23, 1894, to Miss Ethel Wells, the youngest and most charming daughter of A. J. and M. A. Wells, of Wadesboro. She is esteemed for many womanly virtues, a kind heart, and is a true wife in all the word implies. Mr. Hamilton has a bright future before him, bids fair to become one of our most honored and influential citizens, and with pleasure we commend him as an excellent teacher and a high-toned christian gentleman, worthy of the confidence and respect of all with whom he may come in contact.

ELIHU HARRIS,

One of the coming young teachers of the county, was born in  Davidson county, N. C., September 10, 1872. He is the eighth son of T. M. and Sarah Harris, who yet reside in North Carolina. He was raised on the farm until he was seventeen years old, and during this time he only attended school about two months. In 1889 he left his home in the old state and came to Marshall county, Kentucky, and located with his brother, J. L. Harris, in the town of Benton, to whom he is greatly indebted for assisting him in his efforts to educate himself. Since he came to Kentucky he has attended the Marshall County Seminary two terms, and is now teaching an excellent school, at Church Grove, with a good certificate. He is determined to educate himself, and in order to do so he assists his brother in his shop of Saturdays, and in this way pays his board. As soon as his school expires he will enter some high school and continue until he finishes his education. He is sober, moral and possesses fine natural ability, not a member of any church or secret society, but is an old N. C. democrat.

CHARLIE JONES

Was born on the Palmer farm east of the town of Benton, July 4, 1873. He is a son of R. J. and Eliza Jones, who at present reside three miles southeast of Benton. He is of poor parentage and his early education was acquired in the public schools of his neighborhood.  He continued to work on the farm in the summer and attend school in the fall until 1890, he entered the Marshall County Seminary, where he made rapid progress in his studies. In 1894 he again attended the Spring term of the same school in which he distinguished himself as a close student. He passed an examination later in the summer, when he was awarded a first-class certificate. He was given the public school at Salem in district No. 11, in which he taught a most excellent school. He is not a member of any church or secret society, but in politics he is a democrat. He is a very deserving young man and will ultimately make his mark among his fellows.

Professional and Business Men.

DR. BENJAMIN T. HALL

Was born near Symsonia, Graves county, Ky., November 2, 1852. His parents, John and Rebecca B. Hall, came to Kentucky from Davidson county, North Carolina, in 1846, and settled on a farm in Graves county, where they resided until their death, in 1886. The subject of this sketch being their youngest son, received a good English education in the common schools of the county. In 1870 he began the study of medicine under Dr. S. J. Mathews, now of Mayfield, and graduated at the Eclectic Medical Institution, in Cincinnati, Ohio, in May, 1876, and on October 4th, of the same year he was married to Miss Maggie L. Pryor, a grand daughter of Gen. Arthur Davis. They have four daughters, Linnie F., Mintie L., Lizzie and Lena B., aged respectfully 15, 13, 11 and 5. He joined Mt. Pisgah Baptist church in Graves county in 1884 and was ordained to the ministry in December, 1889, and is now pastor of the church at Benton and at New Bethel. Since his graduation in medicine he has been enjoying a good local practice, and is now local surgeon of the P., T. & A. railroad. He is a Mason, an Odd Fellow, and a member of the democratic party. He resides in Benton and is highly respected for his many social and christian traits of character. He has recently been elected trustee of the Marshall County Seminary.

DR. EDMUND G. THOMAS

Was born in Mayfield, Kentucky, June 14, 1852. His parents, J. S. and E. J. Thomas, resided at Mayfield during the boyhood of their son, Edmund, who was the oldest of nine children, where they gave him the best educational advantages that were convenient in his native town. It was by the self-denial of these good parents that the subject of this sketch was blessed with the many advantages he received at their hands in preparing him for a life of success and usefulness. Soon after he was old enough he began the study of medicine, and at the end of his second session in the Medical Department of the University of Louisville, he graduated with the honors of his class in 1873. He came to Marshall county, upon his return from college, and located four miles west of Benton, where he now resides. He has given his entire time to the practice of his profession since he began it, and has made it quite a success. He was married to Miss Cartha Belle Wood, the youngest child of Josiah Wood, on October 5, 1876, by Elder T. F. Harrison. Seven children have blessed this union, four of whom are now living—three boys and one girl. He is a member of the Christian church, and a democrat in politics, serving for years as one of the county committeemen. He is doing a lucrative practice, has an elegant home, and is enjoying life with his happy and contented family.

DR. R. H. STARKS

Was born near Wadesboro, Marshall county, Ky., August 19, 1852.  He is a son of Spencer P. and Mary A. Starks. He was raised on a farm and attended the public schools near his home until he was 17 years old, when he entered the Marshall County Seminary, at Benton, and afterwards taught a few of the public schools of the county. His first business experience was as clerk in the drug store of Dr. A. Smith, in May, 1875, at Benton, with whom he studied medicine. In January, 1877, he entered the Louisville Medical College, from which he graduated in 1878 and returned home and began the practice of medicine at Wadesboro, where he remained one year, at the end of which he came to Benton, where he engaged in the practice of medicine, and also in the drug business. He has continued in the drug business and the practice of his profession until the present. He was in partnership with J. R. Lemon for five years in the drug business, under the firm name of Starks & Lemon, but on October 1, 1890, sold his interest in the store to his partner, and has since been engaged in business for himself. He was married Aug. 18, 1880, to Miss Izora, daughter of J. H. Strow. She died of typhoid fever March 22, 1882. Oct. 20, 1884, he was married to Miss Clara Strow; three children have been born to them, two of whom are now living, Julius and Oda. He was appointed postmaster at Benton Jan. 27, 1890, under President Harrison, and held it until July 1, 1893. He is a K. of H., and a clever and useful citizen.

DR. V. A. STILLEY

Was born at New Concord, Calloway county, Ky., May 19, 1866; he was the oldest son of John M. and S. E. Stilley, and came with his parents to Marshall county in 1873. He received a good English education at the Marshall County Seminary, in 1885 graduated in the Commercial Business College at Evansville, Ind. He returned home and soon afterward began the study of medicine under that learned physician and surgeon, J. W. Johnson. He applied himself very closely to his studies until 1888, when he entered the Medical Department of the University of Louisville, Ky., where he graduated in 1890, after which he returned home and began the practice of his profession among the friends of his boyhood, where he is at present located and is doing a lucrative practice. He was married June 4, 1890, to Miss Katie E. Strow, the only daughter of T. J. Strow, of Benton, Ky. Two children Mary and Marshal, have blessed this marriage, and of course contribute largely to the domestic pleasure and happiness of this interesting family. Doctor Stilley is a member of the Methodist church, an Odd Fellow, and a sound democrat. He is young, studious and energetic, and is destined to be at the head of his profession.

JAMES M. JOHNSON

Was born near Hamlet, Marshall county. Ky., Nov. 26, 1856.

He is the second son of W. H. and Huldah J. Johnson. He was raised on a farm and educated in the common schools of the county. Was married February 22, 1881, to Miss Augusta Heath, a daughter of H. M. Heath. Six children blessed this union, all of whom are now living. He was a successful farmer until 1891, when he retired from the business and took an interest in the Wadesboro Roller Mills, where he remained with his family for two years, making the business quite a success. In January, 1894, he bought property and moved to Benton, where he erected the magnificent Benton Roller Mills, of which he is owner and proprietor. He is an Odd Fellow and a democrat, and believes in the doctrines of the Christian church. He is a popular gentleman and is highly honored and respected by all who know him.

DR. E. T. DUNAWAY

Was born in Arcadia, near Paducah, McCracken county, Ky., in 1860. At eight years of age he was left an orphan boy, and the stern realities and responsibilities of life were upon him. He was thoughtful, industrious and energetic and by and with these most excellent traits of character he acquired for himself a good English education. No higher honor can be given a boy than he can gain for himself, by hard work and close economy and thereby educate and prepare himself for useful citizenship in his native country, as the subject of this sketch has done. He had an ambition to become learned in the practice of medicine, and though an orphan boy, and poor, he soon became able to buy a medical library, from which he soon gained information enough to attend the University of Louisville, from which he graduated with becoming honors in 1893. He returned home and located in the southeast part of Marshall county, near Brewer's Mill, where he now enjoys an honorable practice and implicit confidence of his neighbors. In 1879 he was married to Miss M. V. Phelps, of Calloway, county, and after living happily together for several years she died, April 18, 1888, since which time he has given his time exclusively to the practice of his profession. He is a close student and well versed in the choice literature of the times. He is moral, enterprising and public spirited, and never allows any one to outdo him in the advancement of the public interest.

DR. HORACE NEWTON ROBERTSON

Was born near Calvert City, Marshall county., January 1, 1870. He is a son of T. M. Robertson, one of the largest and most successful farmers in that part of the county. He was raised on the farm until he was fourteen years old, when his father sent him two years to the city schools of Paducah, after which he returned home and remained on the farm until 1887, when he entered the West Kentucky Normal College, at South Carrolton, Ky., where he graduated with all the honors of his class, in 1888. While at school he began the study of medicine, under Doctor Irvin, of that place, but came home and pursued his studies for one year, after which he entered the Kentucky School of Medicine, Louisville, Ky., where he graduated in medicine and surgery June 17, 1891. He then returned home and began the practice of his profession, where he is now engaged with good succeess. He was married September 21, 1892, to Miss Lee Barnes. He is a young man with bright prospects before him, a member of the Marshall County Medical Society, and it is only a matter of time before he will be one of the leading lights of his profession.

PETE ELY

Was born one mile west of Benton, Marshall county, Kentucky,

September 1, 1855, and is a son of W. B. and Susan Ely. Was raised in town and educated in the common schools; was married to Miss Mary E. Barnes May 7, 1879, and six children are the result of this union, three of which are now living. On January 17, 1890, he was appointed jailer, by county Judge E. Barry, to fill out the unexpired term of Jesse A. Lindsey. He was nominated by the democrats of the county for the same office April 5, 1890, and was elected August 4th, following, over James Duncan, independent; was renominated March 10, 1894, and on November 6th, following was re-elected over J. H. Goheen, populist, by 335 majority. His present term of office will expire January 1, 1898. He has always been an active and successful speculator in horses, mules and other live stock, and is at present a large dealer in the same. He began life without a dollar, and it has been by close economy and prudent business sagacity that he is now in good financial condition, and is one of the prominent men of the county. He is not a member of any church, belongs to the Odd Fellows, and is a true democrat.

JOSEPH H. LITTLE

Was born in Henry county Tennessee seven miles east of Paris  August 1, 1850. He was a son of Isaac N. and Francis Little both of whom died when he was very young. He was raised about as a hired hand on a farm, without attending school one day until he was sixteen years old; when he came as a penniless boy to Marshall county, Ky., arriving in September 1866, and began farm work in the neighborhood of Sharpe, where he remained until he was 21 years of age, when he began farming for himself. Notwithstanding he never attended school but 63 days in his life, he has been successful in all of his undertakings. He joined the Cumberland Presbyterian church, in 1870, of which he is still a member; was soon made president of the Marshall County Sunday School Union, a position he has held ever since. He was made a Mason in 1872, has represented his lodge in the Grand Lodge of Kentucky four times, and is now master of the Briensburg lodge; was also a charter member of Benton lodge No. 282, I. O. O. F., of which he is now District Deputy. He was married to Miss Ida Blewett, August 22, 1883, and three children, Thomas, Beulah and Ruby May, have blessed this union. Was elected Sheriff of Marshall county in August 1888, over W. M. Foust, E. C. Dycus, D. A. Lovett and J. R. Lemon, democrats; was re-elected over J. C. Jones, an independent democrat, in 1890; was appointed Master Commissioner, by Judge W. S. Bishop, March 1893, which position he now holds. On March 10, 1894 he received the democratic nomination at a primary election for sheriff, over C. H. Starks and G. W. Parrish. Mr. Starks failed to abide the result of the primary and ran as an independent, and was defeated at the November election by Mr. Little by a majority of 316. He will enter upon the duties of his office January 1, 1895, and hold it for three years. He owns a fine residence in Benton, 300 acres of good farming land near Palma, and stock in the Bank of Benton, of which he is one of the directors. He is a moral, upright, christian gentleman, and is very popular among the people of the county.

J. M. BEAN.

Was born in the southwest part of Marshall county on May 2, 1864. He is the second and youngest son of W. A. and N. A. Bean. He was raised on the farm and educated in the common

schools of the county until he was nearly grown, when he attended part of a session of the Mayfield High school. Afterwards he would work on the farm, and teach school for a living, until 1888, when he came to Benton and began the study of law under Hon. W. M. Reed. At the June term of the Marshall circuit court, 1888, he was examined and a law license given him by R. P. Quarles and H. M. Heath. On August 11, 1889 he was married, in the church at Benton, by Rev. H. C. Gamble, to Miss Maude Woods, daughter of W. A. Woods; one child, Garvis Edwin, has blessed this marriage. He continued the practice of his profession until April 5, 1890, when he received the democratic nomination for county attorney. He was defeated at the regular election by H. M. Heath, independent democrat. He then formed a partnership in the practice of law with J. M.

Fisher, under the firm name of Fisher & Bean, which was dissolved by mutual consent in 1894. On March 10, 1894, he was nominated by the democrats for County Judge of Marshall county, but was defeated by J. J. Dupriest, the nominee of the populist party, by 51 votes. He joined the M. E. church in 1884, is an Odd Fellow and a democrat. He is a coming young man of the county, and not much time will pass before his services will be sought by the people.

C. H. STARKS

Was born six miles south of Benton, Marshall county, Ky., near old Wadesboro, on January 31, 1857. He is the fourth son of Spencer P. and Mary A. Starks.

He was raised on the farm and educated in the public schools of the county until early in 1877, when he entered the Marshall County Seminary under Prof. R. Hayden as the principal where he remained until the close of the Spring session when he began the public school as teacher at Palma, where he taught two sessions, one in 1877, and the other in 1878. At the close of this school he began merchandising at Palma in a general store with W. R. Truitt as his business partner, where he continued until 1884. In July, 1882, the court of claims elected him to the office of School Commissioner, for the county, for two years, which position he filled to the satisfaction of the court and the people. He was elected high sheriff of the county in August, 1884, and re-elected in 1886; his term of office expiring January 1, 1889, and his services were so satisfactory to the people as a good officer that they elected him again to the same position at the November election in 1892, which office he now holds. He was married November 6, 1879, to Miss Ella C. Dycus, the second daughter of Dr. E. C. and A. G. Dycus, of Palma, Ky. Four children, Rupert M., born October 10, 1880; Jesse E., born January 7, 1883; Helen B., born June 26, 1890, and Emmet E., born June 4, 1892, blessed this union. He is a member of the Christian church, an Odd Fellow and a democrat. As a county official he has always proven himself honest and capable, and given perfect satisfaction to his constituency.

GEORGE W. RILEY

Was born in Yadkin county, N. C., October 12, 1863, where he

lived until 1879, when he came with his parents to Marshall county, Ky., and settled seven miles west of Benton near Oak Level. He was raised on a farm and educated in the best public schools of his neighborhood. He, however, soon acquired a good business education. His parents lived in the county for two years, after which they moved one mile west of Oak Level, in Graves county. His father died September 1, 1885, heavily involved in debt for land, and it was by the industry and energy of his son, George, that the indebtedness was liquidated. On December 3, 1888, he left home and erected a distillery at a spring, on the land of Mrs. Henry Reed, in which he and W. H. Reed began the manufacture of white corn whiskey. The business was continued under the firm name of Riley and Reed until January 1, 1890. He came to Benton February 19, 1890, where he sold "still house whiskey" by the quart, until February 19, 1892, when the copartnership of Riley and Reed was dissolved, when he took an interest with E. T. Harper in a still house at Clear Springs, Graves county, where Harper & Riley conducted a partnership business until December 1, 1892, when this firm was dissolved. In December, 1892, he opened up a fine saloon on the historic lot upon which was once located the law office of the lamented J. C. Gilbert, in the town of Benton, where he is now doing a profitable business. He was married February 13, 1890, to Miss Ada Boaz, a daughter of Joshua Boaz, who resides near Hard Money, Ky. Mr. Riley is a young man, in the prime of life, with fine business attainments and ranks high among his acquaintances as a gentleman of honor and integrity.

JOSEPH F. BRANDON

Was born in the town of Benton, Marshall county, Ky., March 7, 1851. He is a son of John W. and Sarah C. Brandon. He was raised in Benton, but never attended school but little, in  fact not more than one year in his life. His father died when he was quite young, and he being the oldest boy, had to give most of his time in providing for the family. In 1873 he began to work for himself, and until 1878 he devoted his time to farming, wool-carding, ginning cotton, etc.. In 1878 he was elected jailer of Marshall county and served until September, 1882. He began business with J. C. McLeod in 1883 and continued until 1886, when he sold his interest, and in 1887 began the grocery and provision business with his brother, George W. Brandon, under the firm name of J. F. Brandon & Bro., in which he is still engaged. On June 25, 1879, he was married to Miss Susan A. Brown, and unto them have been born seven children, six of whom are living, four girls and two boys. Joined the Baptist church in 1865, is a K. of H., Odd Fellow and City Councilman. He is the oldest native born citizen now living in Benton.

W. MIKE OLIVER

Was born seven miles northwest of Benton and near "Old New Hope church," March, 12, 1866. He is a son of James N. and Mary E. Oliver. His father, like most farmers in this county, was a poor man and unable to give his children any educational advantages more than the public schools of his neighborhood. He attended these schools until he was twelve years old, but during the next three years he was kept at home at work on the farm. At the age of fifteen he left home and was employed

as a work hand on the farm of Robert McCain at $8 per month, and it was from his small earnings that he was enabled to go to school and continue his studies, until he began to teach at the age of nineteen, when he taught his first school at Brazzeel's school-house, two miles west of Benton. He continued teaching for 47 months, but in the meantime he completed his education at the S. N. S. & B. College, at Bowling Green, Ky after which he returned home, and in 1888, began the study of law under Hon. W. M. Reed, and was admitted to the bar June 12, 1890. He at once formed a partnership with W. M. Reed, his old preceptor, under the firm name of Reed & Oliver, who practice in all the courts of the state, and is now one of the ablest law firms in Western Kentucky. He is a member of the Christian church. Mr. Oliver was married to Mrs. Lucy V. Palmer December 24, 1892, and they are now living happily together in their new home on Main street. He is a strong democrat and takes considerable interest in local politics. He is, in the truest sense of the word, a self-made man, and it is justly said of him that he is the hardest worker in his profession —he is rarely ever idle. He has recently associated himself with Pete Ely, who is known all over the county for his hustling qualities, and the name of their new firm is Ely & Oliver, Real Estate and Commission agents, which is a step in advance of the general order of things in Marshall; a new adventure. However, we predict for them in their wide-awake efforts, a prosperous business. The subject of this sketch is a student, often burning midnight oil while his neighbors sleep, and in this way is laying up a store of valuable information in many channels. His sober and industrious habits guarantee to him a brilliant future.

GEORGE W. BRANDON

Was born in the town of Benton, Marshall county, Ky., March 13, 1855. He is the second son of John W. and Sarah C. Brandon. His education is quite limited, he never having attended only the common schools, except five months to the Marshall County Seminary. He was married June 25, 1879, to Miss Amelia M. Nelson, daughter of A. A. Nelson, deceased. Three children blessed this marriage, two of whom are now living, Minnie M. and Carmen L. Their mother died on May 3, 1886. Mr.

Brandon has never married again, but lives with his aged mother. He engaged in the grocery and provision business with his brother, J. F. Brandon, in May, 1887, under the firm name of J. F. Brandon & Bro. He joined the Christian church in 1872, and has remained a devoted member ever since. He is an Odd Fellow, a charter member of the K. of H. lodge and a democrat. There is no better citizen in the county; he is mild, modest, honest and enterprising, and highly honored by all who know him.

MARTIN B. COOPER

Was born February 3, 1862, one mile west of Canton, Trigg county, Ky. He is the youngest son of Benjamin and Julia A. Cooper. At nine years old he came with his parents and located near Palma, Marshall county. He was raised on the farm and attended the public schools of his community, and at the age of 22 he became a partner with his brother, Geo Cooper, in a general store at Palma, where he continued until October 1, 1888, when he moved to Benton and engaged in the dry goods business with Emmet C. Dycus. After the termination of this partnership he began the clothing, boot and shoe business with C. H. Starks as his partner under the firm name of Starks & Cooper, of which firm he is still a member. On Sept. 2, 1885, he was married to Miss Mollie A. Dycus, the youngest daughter of Dr. E. C. Dycus. Three children blessed this union, two of whom are living, Earle Y. and Carrie. In June, 1891, he was elected member of the city council; was re-elected in 1892 and again in 1893; his present term will expire January 1, 1896. Is a member of the Board of Trustees of the Marshall County Seminary. He joined the M. E. church in May 1893; belongs to no secret society; is a democrat in politics.

JULIUS L. HARRIS.

The subject whose name appears at the head of this article was born in Davidson county, North Carolina, September 15, 1868. He is the eighth child of T. M. and Sarah Harris, who at present reside in that state. His educational advantages, when a boy, were very poor indeed, and his education of course is very limited, but he inherited from his parents a good stock of common sense, a robust constitution and an indomitable energy. He was not content to spend his life among the rocky hills and the worn-out valleys of his native state, and on March 9, 1889, he landed at Benton, Marshall county, Kentucky. He spent one year on a farm, and on October 6, 1889, he was married to Miss Ella Russell at Oak Level, Kentucky. He came to Benton and began the barber business July 1, 1891, to which he has given his attention ever since, and is now known to be one of the best barbers in all this country. He joined the M. E. Church South November 20, 1892, of which he is a faithful and consistent member. He belongs to no secret society, but in politics he is an unflinching democrat. He is a successful enterprising business man, whose honesty and integrity is never questioned.

DAVID REEVES

Was born near where Oak Level now stands, in Marshall county, Ky., August 6, 1855. He is the second son of Wm. and Percilla J. Reeves. His mother died when he was seven years old. He was raised on the farm and received a fair English education in the common schools of the county. When he became of age he learned the carpenter's trade and followed it successfully until 1890, when he made an unsuccessful race for the democratic nomination for county assessor, being defeated 17 votes by J. A. Clark. He resumed his trade and continued it until March 1, 1893, when he was sworn in as deputy sheriff under C. H. Starks, which position he now holds. It can be truthfully said of him that he has made a clever and faithful officer. Since 1892 he has been one of the county democratic committeemen and has taken a lively interest in the politics of the county. He is single man and a firm believer in the doctrines of the Primitive Baptist church. It is only a short time until he will be one of the prominent men of the county.

WILLIAM B. HAMILTON

Was born three miles west of Benton, at the place where Jack Vaughn now lives, May 8, 1848.  He is the youngest son of John H. and Eliza Hamilton. His father came to Kentucky when he was a boy, and when he grew to manhood he was married to Miss Eliza, the oldest daughter of Gabriel Washburn, who was the mother of the subject of this sketch. He was raised on a farm with very poor educational advantages, but when he was a man he was married to Miss Sarah M. Smith on November 10, 1869, and six children are the result of this union, four of whom are now living, Claude H., Ruth J., Oddie and Elta. His father being a mechanic he inherited a tact for mechanism, from which he has made of himself one of the best workmen in the county. He moved to Briensburg in 1877, and remained there until December 20, 1891, when he moved to Benton, where he at present resides. He lost his entire possessions by fire on January 11, 1893, consisting of a new dwelling, a two-story storehouse and a two-story shop. But by his energy and close attention to business he has rebuilt and is now doing a fine business both in the millinery store and in the carriage and blacksmith shops. He is a member of the Methodist church, and in politics a populist. Mr. Hamilton is a useful citizen and he and his interesting family are well beloved by their neighbors and acquaintances.

DANIEL F. FISER

Was born in Weakly county, Tenn., July 2, 1868, and came with his father and family to Calloway county, Ky., in 1873. He attended the common schools of his neighborhood until 1887 when he moved with his father to Benton, Marshall county, when he began and carried the U. S. mails for several years between Benton and Paducah. He was principally raised on a farm; his mother died when he was only 13 years old. He was married in early manhood to Miss Lenora E. Bearden, a daughter of the late M. B. Bearden, by the Rev. W. G. Hefley at Paris, Tenn. Four children are the result of this marriage. He worked most of his time in prizing and rehandling tobacco until he was elected City Marshal for the town of Benton, which position he still holds. He is the first man that ever made, for the town, a satisfactory town marshal. He is not a member of any church or secret society, but is a true and faithful member of the democratic party. Mr. Fiser is an honest, high toned gentleman.

DAN F. FISER.

W. H. FLEMING

Was born in Murray, Calloway county, Ky., November 26, 1849. He was the oldest son of Josephus and Martha A. Fleming, and moved with them in 1865 to the eastern part of Graves county. During this time he worked on the farm and now and then attended the common schools. On August 6, 1866, he was married in Graves county, to Miss Jane Woods, who became the mother of seven children, three of whom are now living. In October, 1881, he moved to Benton where he has made his home ever since.

After locating in Benton he spent a few years working at a saw and grist mill, but afterwards entered the photograph business at which he is now successfully engaged. He was married on December 13, 1882, to Miss George A. Doublin and seven children blessed this union, five of whom are now living. He belongs to no church or secret society, nor has ever held an office. In politics he is a true and tried democrat and never scratches his ticket.

D. CLINTON STROW,

The second son of T. J. and Clay W. Strow, was born in Benton, Marshall county, Ky., August 7, 1870. He was almost raised in his father's store, and educated in the Marshall County Seminary. He has an excellent English education, but his business course was completed in 1888, when he attended the Bryant & Stratton Business College, Louisville, Ky., where he received a diploma, showing that his advancement was more rapid than that of his classmates. He returned home and soon became the junior member of the well-known mercantile firm of T. J. Strow & Sons, exclusive dealers in Clothing and Gents Furnishing Goods. He is an active, energetic and honorable young man, and is fast pushing himself to the front, as the best business young man in his native town. His firm carries a $10,000 stock of goods, and is doing a large and lucrative business. Their house is located next door to the Bank of Benton. He is a member of the M. E. Church and a good democrat; is unmarried and not a member of any secret society. He sticks close to business, except when he is fishing and hunting, a character of sport of which he is particularly fond.

WALTER G. DYCUS

Was born in Benton, Marshall county, Ky., January 20, 1862. He is the only son of John W. and Greenville Dycus. His mother died when he was one day old, when he was taken and raised by his grandmother, Mrs. Martha P. Ford, with whom he  yet lives and cares for in her old age. He entered the Marshall County Seminary when quite young, and continued therein until he was advanced in all the branches of the common schools. He took a course in Book-keeping under Prof. W. H. F. Henry at Sharpe, Ky., and in 1882–3 he attended ten months at Clinton College. He spent several years in teaching the common schools of Marshall and Hickman counties, from 1880 to 1889, teaching in all 35 months. He was appointed deputy county clerk Dec. 3, 1877, under T. L. Goheen, jr., with whom he learned the duties of that office, and continued to perform them until the death of Mr. Goheen, in October, 1880. In 1885 was appointed deputy clerk in the same office under W. J. Wilson. On June 11, 1885 he was made deputy circuit clerk, under the lamented T. F. Palmer, and was re-appointed to the same position on December 22, 1890, under Solon L. Palmer, which place he filled until his term of office expired. He was defeated for county clerk in 1886 by W. J. Wilson, and again by the same man in 1890; in the last race Mr. Wilson ran as an independent democrat and Mr. Dycus as the nominee of the democratic party. On March 10, 1894, he received the democratic nomination for county clerk, over nine worthy opponents, and was elected on November 6, 1894, over J. Hardin Ford, his republican opponent, by 420 majority. He was appointed deputy under Mr. Wilson on November 20, 1894, and will continue in the office until January 1st, when he will be installed as clerk. He was appointed by Judge C. L. Randle as examiner to take depositions June 25, 1887. He joined the M. E. Church South in August, 1881, and is yet a consistent member of the same. Is Secretary of the Marshall County Sunday School Union, and has been several times a delegate to the State Union. Was elected President of District No. 2, at Russellville, August, 1894. He joined the Good Templars, at the age of 13, and has kept his pledge ever since. Is a charter member of Benton lodge No. 282, Odd Fellows, that was organized April 7, 1888, and has attained the highest degrees in subordinate lodges; has represented his lodge twice in the Grand Lodge of the State, and is a member of Ingleside Rebecca lodge No. 17, Paducah, Ky. He has held several other places of honor and trust, and will hold many more, for he is a young man with bright promises before him.

R. B. HEATH

Was born near Briensburg, Marshall county, Kentucky, Dec. 8, 1860, and is the fifth son of P. J. and Ada A. Heath. He was

raised on the farm, and attended school but very little, until he was 18 years old when he left Kentucky and moved to Sumpter county, Florida, where he remained until 1883, when he returned to Kentucky and located in Graves county, where he remained for three years. He was married Oct. 9, 1884, to Miss Jane Shoat, of Graves county. Four children have been born to them, two of whom are now living, Mertie E. and Cora L. He came to Marshall county in 1888, and worked on a farm until 1891, when he became a citizen of Benton, where he now resides. In the early part of 1894 he was appointed deputy city marshal, which position he now holds. On November 6, 1894, he was elected city marshal for a term of two years, over two competent opponents. He will enter upon the discharge of of his official duties January 1, 1895. In belief he is a Methodist, and in politics a democrat. He attends closely to his own business, and has recently become very popular as a brave and chivalrous officer. He is a conservative gentleman and a terror to the violators of the law.

HON. W. M. REED

Was born in Graves county, Kentucky, September 5, 1848; is the second son of William and Margaret Reed, his father being killed by a falling tree before he was born. His mother  afterwards married Noah Park, who was a farmer, and it was on the farm with his parents that he was raised until he was seventeen years old, during which time he attended the public schools of his native community. For three years afterward he would teach school in the fall and go to school in the early part of the year. In 1869 he came to Benton, where he entered the Marshall County Seminary, and remained until it was closed early in 1871, when he attended one session at Princeton College. After his return he began the study of law in 1872 under that able jurist, P. Palmer, and was admitted to the bar in January 1873, after passing a rigid examination by Hon. A. R. Boone and Judge James D. White. He entered upon the practice of his chosen profession in the same year, at his home in Benton, where he has been successfully engaged until the present time. He has done a district practice for several years past and has been engaged in most all the important murder trials in this and adjoining counties. He was young and ambitious and it was not long until he began to take an active part in politics as a democrat. He was appointed county attorney in 1875, and in 1876 was elected to a full term, but in 1877 he resigned his position as county attorney and was elected to the legislature from the counties of Marshall and Lyon. He was again elected to the legislature in 1885-6, and re-elected in 1887-8, when he was a prominent candidate for speaker of the House of Representatives. He was chairman of the Judiciary Committee and a member of the impeachment court that tried James W. Tate for defaulting as State Treasurer. He was only defeated in the state convention by a small majority for delegate from the state at large, to the last National convention. He was not a candidate for the place until after the convention met, which shows his great popularity in the state. As a lawyer of ability he has but few superiors in the state. He has practiced law with several of the best attorneys in Western Kentucky as partners, and is now a member of the well-known law firms of Greer & Reed, of Paducah, and Reed, Greer & Oliver, of Benton. He is attorney for the P., T. & A. Railroad Company, besides several Banks, Trust Companies and other monied corporations. He was married October 17, 1872, to Miss Mary Rosie Strow; five children have been born to them, four of whom are living, Boone, Cecil, Lula and Roscoe. Rubie died in her infancy. Mr. Reed is a member of the Christian church, a Mason, an Odd Fellow, and chairman of the democratic county committee. As a lawyer, a farmer and a politician he stands at the head of the list in this end of the state. He has an elegant home, and possesses valuable property in both Marshall and McCracken counties.

JOHN T. LENTS

Was born November 14, 1847, in Marshall county, Ky., three miles south of Benton. He is a son of Davidson and Elizebeth Lents, who were born and raised in Bedford county, Tennessee. His mother was a sister of G. W. Slaughter. His parents died when he was quite young, which left him without the facilities of educating himself, and at the age of seventeen years he was married to Miss Mary A. Hiett, the daughter of J. W. Hiett, and eleven children have been born to them as a result of this union, nine of whom are now living. They have eight grand children, besides a large connection. He has always been a farmer until 1891, when he entered the coffin business, two miles south east of Benton, since which time he has built himself a good trade. In 1888 he joined the Christian church, since which time he has lived a much better life. He was a democrat until 1892, when he joined the populist party and voted for J. B. Weaver, and is now a strong worker for his party's success. He is a good, law-a-biding citizen, and is highly respected by all who know him.

JAMES H. FORD

Was born September 12, 1873. He was the only son of Marion and Ollie Ford who died when he was three years old. He at-

tended the common schools in his district and the Marshall county Seminary at Benton and Murray Institute; but is chiefly indebted for his education to "home study" having been, from infancy, a persistent student of history, both ancient and modern, and English Literature. He began teaching school when seventeen years old at Jackson school house and continued successfully at different places until he arrived at the age of twenty. At the age of 19 he began the Study of Law under the supervision of Dycus & Lovett and has continued it ever since. Obtained license to practice law in October, 1894, just one month after his twenty first birthday. In politics he is a staunch republican, having taken an active part in the cause of his party, both in county and district for several years past. Was nominated by the republican convention, March 12th. for County Court Clerk, although he was defeated he received over 700 votes— twice as many as any republican in the county. Will now enter upon his chosen profession, that of the Law, for the future. He is a close student, a young man of extra ability and the time is not distant when he will be one of the leading men of his profession.

Life of Mrs. W. B. Hamilton.

Mrs. W. B. Hamilton, (nee Smith), wife of W. B. Hamilton, was born in Chapel Hill, Marshall county, Tenn., September 10, 1848. Moved with her parents to Kentucky, when six years old. Has lived in Marshall county, Ky., ever since. Was educated in the public schools in Crittenden, Trigg, Calloway and Marshall counties. Taught school when 18 years of age with a first-class certificate. Was married to W. B. Hamilton Nov. 10, 1869. She with her husband moved to Briensburg, Ky., December 8, 1876, where she lived till January, 20, 1892, when she removed to Benton, Ky., where she now resides. Joined the M. E. church South, August 13, 1864. Began in the millinery business at Briensburg in the spring of 1888. Was at that time the only milliner in the county. Her stock and house was small but by prompt attention to business she has built up the best millinery trade in the county. Opened up business in Benton, Ky., in the spring of 1892. Lost her entire establishment by fire January 11, 1893. Rebuilt the same year on the same ground and is now enjoying a large trade in her line. She is the mother of six children four of whom are living. Her eldest daughter, Ruth has learned her trade as trimmer in the wholesale millinery markets of St. Louis and Louisville.

MRS. HAMILTON'S STORE.

Oak Level.

Oak Level is situated seven miles west of Benton on the Wadesboro and Paducah dirt road. It has never been incorporated, but is a good country business point, surrounded by a clever, hard-working, honest character of people. It has two churches, a Christian and Methodist, one school house, one general store, one drug store, two blacksmith and wagon shops one steam mill, one minister and two physicians. Mr. James Reeves is the postmaster.

ELDER T. F. HARRISON,

The oldest child of Elder B. J. and Mrs. Margaret W. Harrison,

was born in Davidson county, N. C., on September 1, 1839. In the winter of 1845-6 his father moved with his family, in a wagon drawn by three horses, to this county, being about 42 days on the road, encountering rough mountainous roads and winter weather. He, (T. F. H.), was raised on a farm, learned to plow, cut wheat with a scythe and cradle, mow grass with the old fashioned Dutch hammered grass blade, to thresh oats with a hickory frail and raise the wind with a blanket to clean out the chaff, to feed the old "ground hog" thresher; went to district schools usually of three months duration, and in May 1859 obtained a first-class certificate as a qualified teacher of common schools in Marshall county; the said certificate was the result of a close examination by the late Philander Palmer, who was at that time the examiner of common school teachers for said county. Commenced teaching in the common schools in 1859, and continued to farm on a small scale in the summer, and teach in the fall and winter, till 1871, when he became the deputy county surveyor under James G. Haydock, now of Missouri. In 1872, upon Mr. Haydock's resignation, was appointed county surveyor, and served in that capacity for several terms, and is now the county surveyor by appointment to fill the unexpired term of Mr. B. F. Sears, resigned. Was married to Miss Louisa J. Wallace, December 2, 1859, who is now the companion of his riper years. Nine children, 5 of whom are living, and 17 grand children, have been the result of this union. Professed faith in Christ on June 20, 1864, was baptized on the 3rd Sunday in the following July by Elder P. W. Austin, as a member of the Primitive or Regular Baptist church, at Union. Was ordained and clothed with the full functions of a gospel minister on Saturday before the 3rd Sunday in August, 1869, by the following presbytery: Elders P. W. Austin, W. W. Worrell, Bird McKinney, E. Watkins, G. Gibson and B. J. Harrison and deacons John Hall, C. Burkhart, T. R. Bolton and B. Bell. He has labored hard for a living for his family and try to discharge his duty to the church as a preacher. Has been the clerk of the union meetings of Soldier Creek Association for 24 years; has been the clerk of the annual meetings of the Soldier Creek Association for 22 years. Has married more than 400 couples since January 1, 1871, and believes he has married more pretty girls than any preacher now living in the county. He is one of the ablest preachers in his church, and in politics a democrat.

Harvey, Kentucky.

Harvey was founded a few years ago by James H. Ivey, and is situated five miles west of Benton, near Pleasant Grove church. It consists of a general store, postoffice and residence; is not incorporated, nor is it a town, but is a place located in the center of a fine farming country, surrounded by a thrifty, law-abiding people. J. H. Ivey owns the entire place and is the present democratic postmaster. He buys all the produce of the community, and sells large quanties of merchandise to his section of the country.

JAMES H. IVEY

Was born in East Tennessee, October 18, 1830. His parents moved to Rutherford county in 1837. He remained on the farm with his father until 1856, during which time he only attended school six months, and never learned to count interest until he was 45 years old. In 1856 he came to Marshall county, Kentucky, and bought a piece of land of A. A. Nelson one and ahalf miles west of Benton, for $700 cash and $400 on a credit. In Junuary 1857 he returned to Tennessee and was married to Miss Martha Jane Pugh; they returned to his new home in Kentucky, and nine childred blessed this union, five of whom are now living and four dead. In 1880 he left the farm and began merchandising, which is still his occupation. Ten years ago he established the Harvey postoffice and has been its postmaster ever since. He joined the M. E. church in 1855; is a Mason, and in politics he was a Whig until he voted for Bell and Everett, since he has been a democrat. The business life of Mr. Ivey is a worthy example to all young men. He left his father at 21 years old without a dollar, and for five years hired out as a farm hand, and when he came to Kentucky he had saved up $700 in cash. Now he owns 500 acres of land, a brick store house with $3,000 worth of goods, a fine dwelling house, besides stock in four banks and in the Mayfield Woolen mills. He has been truly a successful man in business.

ISAAC WASHAM

Was born October 16, 1836. Received an ordinary education in the common schools of that day. Professed religion and joined the M. E. Church South in 1856. He married Miss Mary P. Ray, daughter of Hicks J. Ray, February 1, 1857. In August, 1862, he joined the United States army, and was honorably discharged in October, 1863. He joined the Masonic order in 1870; in 1878 was elected Justice of the Peace, and in 1882 was re-elected for another full term. Qualified as deputy county court clerk in 1890, and in 1894 was appointed Justice of the Peace to fill out the unexpired term of K. F. Pember, resigned. His many years' service, on the fiscal court of the county, has demonstrated the fact that he is a careful, safe and conservative public servant. He lives in the southwest part of the county on a farm, and is a citizen above reproach. In politics he is a staunch republican.

The Town of Olive.

Olive is situated in the southeast part of the county, seven miles from Benton, and is a very old place. It has one Union church house, one school house, two general stores, one blacksmith shop and about eight dwelling houses. The place was started by J. M. Chandler, who is its oldest resident. L. C. Starks is the young and polite postmaster.

W. A. HARTLEY

Was born in Calloway county, Kentucky, in the year 1853, where he lived until 1862, when he moved with his father to Marshall county. He was raised on a farm, by very poor parents, and had, when a boy, poor educational advantages; in fact, he educated himself, after he arrived at manhood, and was a successful school teacher for twelve years. He has been engaged in merchandising at Olive since January, 1889, with phenominal success. He was married to Miss Melissa Norwood February 2, 1893. One sweet baby girl, Miss Flora, has blessed this union, and was born July 20, 1894. Mr. Hartley is a self-made man, and is highly respected by all who know him.

L. C. STARKS.

The following cut represents a good likeness of Mr. L. C. Starks, the junior member of the firm of R. W. Starks & Son, at Olive and Hardin, Ky., and editor of the Hardin Star. Mr.

Starks was born and raised in Marshall county, and is 23 years old. He was married to Miss Lillie G. Green, daughter of C. M. Green, of Benton, October 23, 1892.; they have one sweet little girl, Winona. The firm of R. W. Starks & Son, of which Mr. Starks is the junior member, is one of the largest concerns in the county, doing twice the amount of business annually of any other firm. When the new town of Hardin was started up they were among the first to erect a handsome new two-story brick business house. Mr. Starks thinking the town ought to have a newspaper, started the publication of the Hardin Star, which has been a decided success. He will enlarge and otherwise improve his paper, on January 1, 1895, having already ordered new machinery, etc., for his plant. Mr. Starks has been very successful in life, and has never undertaken any enterprise but what has been carried out successfully. He is an energetic young business man, and should he live to reach an old age he will, undoubtedly, be one of the prominent men of his native county.

A Sound Institution.

BANK OF BENTON, BENTON, KENTUCKY.

(Incorporated in 1890.)

The Bank of Benton was organized and commenced business September 20, 1890. The financial success of this Bank has been most wonderful; commencing business with a capital stock of $12,500, paid in, it has earned for its stockholders over $7,000, from then until now.

The Bank owns its own banking house, on the west side of the court square, and it is fitted with the latest improved safe and vault. Judge J. W. Dycus is president; J. D. Peterson, vice-president; Solon L. Palmer, cashier. The directors are Judge J. W. Dycus, Capt. J. R. Smith, of J. R. Smith & Co., wholesale grocers, Paducah, Ky., J. D. Peterson, W. A. Holland J. H. Little, R. W. Starks, of Hardin, G. W. Slaughter and R. F. Jenkins.

Every note accepted by this Bank must be well and satisfactorily secured, and that is the reason they can truthfully say that the Bank has never lost a dollar on any note discounted by it. This Bank is one of the most solid financial institutions in this end of the state, and the people of the county are justly proud of it, in having a perfectly safe place to deposit their money, and with whom to transact all of their commercial business.

BANK OF BENTON, BENTON, KENTUCKY.
(Incorporated in 1890.)

J. W. DYCUS, President.   J. D. PETERSON, Vice-President.
SOLON L. PALMER, CASHIER.

LENTS'
UNDERTAKING ESTABLISHMENT.

One mile and a-half Southeast of Benton.

JOHN T. LENTS, PROPRIETOR.

Carries a Full Stock of Coffins, Caskets, Etc.

Full and complete Line of Burial Robes, Etc.

M R. LENTS is one of the county's best business men; and treats his customers well, when dealing with him. His shop is open at all times, day and night, and he is ready and willing to accommodate his friends. If you need anything in his line it will pay to call and see him.

PETE ELY.

Ely & Oliver,

MIKE OLIVER.

Real Estate and Commission Agents.

We buy and sell lands of all kinds in Marshall county. We find purchasers for the lands that you have for sale. We find lands, for those seeking homes, in a good community. We rent lands for nonresident owners of lands, and act for them as they may direct. We solicit correspondence with those who have land for sale. We solicit correspondence with those who wish to buy a new home, just as good as the one you now have, and better, for one half of what you can realize out of the one you now have. We solicit correspondence with those who have a small farm in sections of the country where lands are high, and sell for prices ranging from $15 to $30 per acre, who would like to purchase land just as good, which will produce even more, at prices ranging from $5 to $20 per acre, according to location. Marshall county has some of the best farming lands in the state, which will yield from 40 to 75 bushels of corn per acre, from 800 to 1,500 pounds of tobacco per acre, from 12 to 35 bushels of wheat per acre, from one to two tons of hay per acre, with EXCELLENT RANGE for STOCK; FINE BOTTOM or VALLEY land; RIDGE land; IMPROVED and UNIMPROVED; stock water in abundance. More than 78,000 acres yet in timber; creeks in every community in the county which afford clear running water the whole year. Two railroads running entirely through the county—C. O. & S. W. in the northern part, and the P. T. & A. through the center—eight railroad stations in county; 7 boat landings on Tennessee river in county, which river forms the entire east and north boundary of the county. Fine School system; CHURCHES in Every Community in the county; best of society; High School in Benton, (county seat), ten months in the year. When the natural resources of Marshall county are once developed it is sure to be the Banner county of West Kentucky for agricultural and stock raising purposes. We have the soil which is sure to make it such, and all that is needed is new emigrants who are wide-awake, industrious and energetic enough to utilize what has been given to us by nature's own hand. Average price of lands in Marshall county in 1893 $5.42. Rapidly increasing in price; if you want a good home cheap, either in the country, in a village or in the county seat, now is your time to purchase, for it is growing higher each year.

For further information address us at Benton, Marshall county Ky., and we will cheerfully give you any desired information.

A. H. WEAR.

A. H. Wear & Son.
MURRAY, KENTUCKY.

MANUFACTURERS OF

WEAR'S RHEUMATIC LINIMENT,

GARDNER-ROGERS
COUGH & CONSUMPTION CURE,

Wear's Sarsaparilla,

MELOAN'S STIFLE LINIMENT.
(For Hoses.)

No Grease, Dirt or Slop!

We don't offer a dirty, greasy, sloppy oil as an excuse for a Liniment. Ours is a Liniment sure enough. Made of the very best material—contains no cheap, nasty oils; will not soil or stain the skin, or clothing. Is a nice, clean penetrating Liniment. When applied strikes in and gives relief at once. It is a most excellent Family Liniment. Has been used with success in Rheumatism, Neuralgia, Cramp Colic, Sprains, Bruises, Strains, Swellings, and all kinds of aches and pains in the Stomach and Bowels. Druggists sell it, at 25 and 50 cents per bottle.

That's Right! Let Everybody Know

That the old reliable Gardner-Rogers Cough and Consumption Cure is still enjoying the most excellent reputation it so richly deserves; that of curing Coughs, Colds, Bronchitis, Asthma, and all effections of throat and lungs, where many other remedies have failed entirely. Once a friend to it you will always be—a trial will cost you one dollar, and if you are not benefitted the full dollar's worth the amount

Will Be Refunded.
SOLD BY ALL DRUGGISTS.

DR. WILEY ROGERS is a leading physician of Louisville, Ky., and occupies a prominent place on the Kentucky State Board of Pharmacy. He it was who first made the Gardner-Rogers Cough and Consumption Cure, prescribed it in his practice and afterward bottled and put it on the market, and you may be sure if this remedy had not have been the very best he would have had nothing to do with it. As a cure for coughs, colds, bronchitis, asthma, catarrh, and all throat and lung affections it has no superior, and few equals, if any. Druggists sell it at one dollar a bottle.

OAKLAND ROLLER MILLS,
J. M. WATSON, Proprietor,
SHARPE, KY.

Special Brands: "Omega." "Sunlight."

The proprietor of these mills is a native of Alabama, was raised on a farm and taught school when young. Since he grew to manhood has devoted most of his time to railroading, and has held all positions from brakeman to conductor of the fast mail, from Memphis to Louisville. He is 50 years old, and is a fine business man He has been proprietor of the Oakland Mills for three years, and has built for himself a large and prosperous business.

J. F. Brandon & Brother,

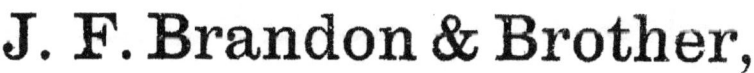
—DEALERS IN—

Staple and Fancy Groceries,

Meats, Seeds, Eggs, Potatoes,

And Country Produce.

South Court Square, Benton, Ky.

"The Old Reliable."

W. A. HOLLAND

——DEALER IN——

DRY GOODS,
NOTIONS,
Dress Goods, Boots,
Shoes, Hats, Caps,

Staple and Fancy Groceries

And Everything usually kept in a First Class General Store.

South Court Square,   Benton, Ky.

BENTON ROLLER MILLS.

J. M. JOHNSON, Proprietor.

Benton, - - - Kentucky.

Exchange 37 pounds flour to bushel of First Class wheat.

Grinding Days, four last days in each week.

J. W. STARKS,

—DEALER IN—

Dry Goods, Notions, Boots

And Shoes, Groceries

Hardware and General Merchandise

Hardin, Kentucky.

"Don't Tobacco Spit or Smoke Your Life Away." The truthful, startling title of a book about No-to-bac, the only harmless, GUARANTEED tobacco-habit cure. If you want to quit and can't, use "No-to-bac." Braces up nicotinized nerves, eliminates nicotine poisons, makes weak men gain strength, weight and vigor. Positive cure or money refunded. Sold by all druggists. Book at druggists, or mailed free. Address The STERLING REMEDY Co., Chicago, office, 45 Randolph Street.; New York, 10 Spruce Street.

DR. R. H. STARKS,

Druggist,

Dealer in

Pure Drugs

and

Medicines

CHOICE PERFUMES
And Fine Toilet
Articles.

Patent Medicines
and
Druggists' Sundries.

PAINTS,

OILS,

BRUSHES
——and——
Painters Supplies.

School Books

STATIONERY
——and——
School - Supplies.

Fine Line
Cigars and Tobacco.

West Side Court Square,

Benton, - - - Kentucky.

J. A. STEPHENS,

Dealer in **WALL PAPER,**

Lead, Paints, Oils, Brushes, Etc

Mr. Stephens was born in Marshall county 35 years ago, and is now one of Benton's best business men. He conducts his business in the house shown above, which is situated next door to T. J. Strow & Sons, west side of court square, where he carries a full and complete stock of Lead, Paints, Oils Brushes, Wall Paper, Picture Frames, etc. He is a nice, polite gentleman, and the public can find no better place to buy such goods as he handles than here. He also carries a good line of Confectioneries, candies, fruits, etc. The public is cordially invited to call and see him.

LEADING BRANDS
Kentucky & Tennessee Whiskies

BELLE MONROE
3 to 5 yrs old

BELLE NELSON
3 to 5 yrs old

ROBERTSON COUNTY
3 to 5 yrs old

LINCOLN CO.
2 to 6 yrs old

GUCKENHEIMER RYE
3 to 5 yrs old

OLD ED TAYLOR
6 years old

OLD LOG CABIN
3 to 5 yrs old

O. F. C.
12 years old in bottle

J. W. McCULLOCH GREEN RIVER
3 to 5 yrs old

THE ABOVE FINE WHISKIES

Are For Sale by

G. W. RILEY,

West Side Court Square,

Benton, Kentucky.

Fergerson & Rowe.

THE ONLY
Hardware Store
In the County.

Complete Stock of **Harrows, Cultivators, Plows, Wagons, Carts,** STOVES, HINGES, LOCKS, ETC WIRE.

Pocket and Table Cutlery.

Harness : and : Saddlery

West Side Square, Benton, Ky.

NAT RYAN

Wide Awake and up to the Times

⇒Clothier ✦ Furnisher⇐

——AND——

General Dry Goods Merchant

Hardin, Kentucky.

Buy For Cash. ✳ Sell For Cash.

E. ZUECKLER,

——DEALER IN——

Drugs, Patent Medicines,

Toilet Articles,

Druggists' Sundries, Etc.

Birmingham, Kentucky.

☞ Physicians' Prescriptions Carefully Compounded.

J. D. PETERSON'S CASH GROCERY.

THE above is a true picture of the business house now owned and occupied by J. D. PETERSON, one of Benton's enterprising citizens. He began the Grocery business here in the year 1882, and has continued up to the present time, and is now doing a good business in his line. He carries a nice line of Staple and Fancy Groceries, Flour, Lime, Salt, Cement, etc., a Full stock of Farming Implements and Garden and Field Seeds of all kinds. He has built up a good trade, by being honest and dealing fair with the people, and now enjoys the confidence and esteem of his customers. Mr. Peterson is one of the county's best business men.

BARRY & STEPHENS

—DEALERS IN—

Pure Drugs and Medicines,

Groceries, Hardware, Etc.

Benton - Kentucky.

FULTON HOUSE

Mrs. Jas. Love, Proprietress

Birmingham, Ky

Good Sample Rooms for Commercial Men.

J. M. Fisher,

Attorney-at-law

BENTON, KY.

Will practice in the United States court at Paducah, and in all the State courts of Ky. Special Attention given to Collection.

Fleming's Art Gallery,

W. H. FLEMING, Proprietor,

Benton, - Kentucky.

Fine Photographs, Tintypes, Etc.

Old Pictures Copied and Enlarged.

T. H. HALL & COMPANY

—DEALERS IN—

Dry Goods, Boots and Shoes

Hats and Caps,

FANCY NOTIONS, ETC.

West Side Square, Benton, Ky.

W. B. Hamilton,

Wagon and Carriage Maker.

Benton, Kentucky.

All Kinds **Blacksmithing** AND **Repairing** DONE

New Ground Plows

A Specialty

W. M. REED,   W. D. GREER,   W. M. OLIVER,
Benton, Ky.   Paducah, Ky.   Benton, Ky.

Reed, Greer & Oliver,
Lawyers.

Will practice in the Federal and State courts at Paducah, Ky., and in the courts of Marshall, Livingston, Calloway, Graves and adjoining counties.

—

Special Attention given to Collection.

ATTORNEYS FOR

Paducah, Tennessee & Alabama Railroad Company.

—

OFFICES:

PADUCAH, KENTUCKY.

AND

BENTON, KENTUCKY.

Hardin Grocery Company,
Ed. S. SLEDD, Manager.
Staple and Fancy Groceries.
Hardin,   Kentucky.

JOHN G. LOVETT

Attorney-at-Law and County Attorney for Marshall Co. Ky.

Practice in all the Courts, State and Federal. Prompt Attention Given to Collection.

OFFICE IN COURT HOUSE, BENTON, KENTUCKY.

T. E. BARNES,

—DEALER IN—

Dry Goods, Notions, Boots

Fancy Millinery,

Shoes, Hats, Caps and Furniture.

Benton   -   Kentucky.

Mrs. W. B. Hamilton,

DEALER IN

Fashionable

AND

FANCY MILLINERY.

—o—

Hats Trimmed

TO ORDER.

BENTON, - KENTUCKY.

W. J. WILSON & SON,

Successors to J. R. Lemon,

——DEALERS IN——

Drugs, Paints, Oils, Etc.,

School Books,

Tobacco, Cigars and Pipes.

Benton, Kentucky.

INDEX

-A-

Abshinn, Dr. 72
Agner, Peter 7
Alford, Joe 42
Anderson, G. W. 51
    Irvin 34
    W. M. 63, 68
    W. R. 53
Arant, Alzada E. 77
    Felix A. 77
    Hugh 38
Ashworth, James 8
Atwood, W. G. 48
Austin, P. W. 137
    Wat 39
Averitt, John J. 37

-B-

Baker, Glover 8
    James 8
    William 7
Barnes, George F. 40
    Lee 117
    Mary E. 117
    T. E. 37, 40, 159
    Thomas E. 37
Barnett, J. T. 92
    L. T. 38
    Marques 38
Barnhart, Jennie 109
    Joshua 38, 108
    Mariah 108
    William 63, 108-9
Barry, E. 37, 53, 58, 117
    Elias 35, 38
    Jackson 53
Bean, Garvis Edwin 119
    J. M. 81, 85, 119-20
    L. I. 63
    Maude 119
    N. A. 119
    W. A. 119
Bearden, Lenora E. 128
    Lucy 64
    M. A. 63
    M. B. 128
Beckham, P. H. 10
    Pleasant H. 35
Beech, Mr. 7

Belcher, C. A. 50
Bell, B. 137
    James 45
Belt, Captain 40
Benbrook, Mr. 7
Benson, E. W. 109
Benton, Thomas H. 79
Bibb, Mr. 7
Bigger, J. M. 33
Bishop, W. S. 118
Blewett, Ida 118
    T. H. 90
Boaz, Ada 122
    Joshua 122
Bolton, T. R. 48, 137
Bond, C. B. 42
Bondurant, T. E. 53
Boone, A. R. 132
Bourland, Hiram 49
    James 7
    Lucinda 55
Bowerman, Milton 39
Bowman, Nathan 44
Boyd, Alfred 4, 33
    Anna 100
    Artely 99
    J. M. 99
    Linn 10
    Robert Clinton 99-100
Bradshaw, W. F. 85
Bramlet, Governor 42
Brandon, Amelia M. 124
    Carmen L. 124
    G. W. 58
    George W. 122, 124
    J. F. 37, 58, 124, 147
    John W. 122, 124
    Joseph F. 122
    Minnie M. 124
    Sarah C. 122, 124
    Susan A. 122
Brank, James 8
Brannock, J. P. 50, 63, 64
Brazel, Jacob 51
Brewer, Elizabeth 53
    J. M. P. 53
Brian, Dr. 72
Brien, James 4, 9, 10, 33, 96
Brown, Governor 109
    C. M. 91
    David 108

Brown, Depue 91
    Hugh 53
    James 7
    James L. 91
    John 8
    Mahala 108
    Sarah Jane 108
    Smith 49
    Susan A. 122
    T. D. 53, 63, 68, 108, 109
    William 7
Buford, Lucy A. 81
Bullitt, W. G. 82, 84
Burkhart, C. 137
Burnham, James 50
Burradell, F. 26
    Frank 23
Butler, W. L. 53

-C-

Calvert, P. W. 102
Campbell, Judge 103
    Alexander 45, 104
    John 8
    M. 8
Cardwell, C. E. 94
Carl, J. S. 51, 52
Carney, Robert 7
Carson, Mr. 49
Carter, Thomas 40
Cason, T. F. 50, 51
Castleberry, N. S. 56, 57, 75
Chambers, William 11
Champion, Willis 105
Chandler, J. M. 139
Childs, J. L. 37
Chiles, W. T. 33
Clark, J. A. 38, 126
    J. T. 63
    James 4
    Robert 37
    W. H. 101
Clayton, F. 48
    F. H. 48, 49
    Francis 43, 79
    Francis H. 4
    Moses 7
Cole, Emma 82
Coleman, Clemmie 89
    T. C. 71
Collie, D. H. 50

Collie, Elijah 49
    W. F. G. 53
Condrum, Isaac 8
Cooper, Benjamin 125
    Carrie 125
    Earle Y. 125
    George 125
    Julia A. 125
    M. B. 50
    Martin B. 125
    Mollie A. 125
Cope, Spencer 64
Copeland, Absalom 45
    N. 48
    Sally 48
    W. H. 42
Coulter, C. C. 34, 38, 83, 84
Covington, Victoria J. 53
Cox, Mr. 28
Cross, A. E. 63
Crossland, Ed. 42, 76
Crow, E. 55
Crowell, D. B. 63
Cummins, W. M. 7
Curd, Edmund 12

-D-

Daniel, Mr. 7
Darnall, Benjamin 11
    H. 49
    Harry 10, 48
    Henry 7, 10-11, 12, 45, 60
    N. 98
    Nicholas 11, 35
    Phillip 35, 37
    Polly 11
    William 11
Darnold, William 8
Davidson, Charles B. 4
Davis, Mr. 7
    Arthur 112
    Arthur H. 7, 11-12
    C. D. 52
Dees, Sam 42
Dillard, Edward 7
Dinwiddie, Samuel 7
Dishman, Ewing 46
Dodd, Colonel 10
    Henry 36
Dooms, Jack 8
Doon, M. 8

Doublin, George A. 129
Draffen, Emma 65
    John T. 63, 65
Dunaway, E. T. 116
    M. V. 116
Duncan, James 117
    Samuel 37, 40
    Velina 60
Dunn, Mr. 8
    E. J. 50
    Elizabeth 50
    Farrar 49
    G. W. 50
    Joseph 49
    Julia A. 72
    William 42
Dupriest, J. J. 50, 120
    John B. 42
    John Bunyan 80
    John J. 35, 42, 80-1
    Lucy A. 81
    Mary P. 81
    Matilda W. 80
    Robert L. 81
Dycus, Dr. 72
    Judge 86
    A. G. 121
    E. C. 71, 118, 121
    Ella C. 121
    Emmet C. 125
    Greenville 130
    J. W. 33, 35, 36, 38, 50, 85, 141, 142
    John W. 36, 130
    Mollie A. 125
    Walter G. 130-1

-E-

Earley, William 8
Eaton, James 7
Edwards, Crittenden 39
    G. C. 63
    J. E. 46
    John 42
    W. H. 53
Eggner, N. A. 77
Elliott, Elnathan 39
    John 69
    John R. 69
    Matilda 69
    Robert 4
    T. N. 69

Elliott, W. H. 63
    William 46
    William Henry 69
Ellis, Ira 33
Ely, Ida 84
    Jack 84
    Mary E. 117
    Pete 37, 117, 124, 144
    Susan 117
    W. B. 35, 37, 117
English, Elizabeth 103, 104
    Maude M. 104
    Ruth A. 104
    Thomas W. 104
    W. W. 37, 88, 103-4
Entrikan, John 7
Etheridge, Mrs. 41

-F-

Faircloth, Ellie 101
Faughn, Enos 4, 37
    James 8
    John 8
Fickline, Joseph 95
Fields, Alice 97
    J. Louis 97
    John W. 90
    Lizzie 97
    Louis 38
    Nancy E. 90
    Samantha A. 90
    W. R. 90
Finch, Jack 54
    Polly 54
Finley, Elizabeth 55
    L. E. 71, 102-3
    Willie P. 102
Finney, R. P. 51
Fiser, Daniel F. 127-8
    Lenora E. 128
Fisher, Ida 84
    J. M. 36, 38, 64, 110, 119, 120, 156
    James M. 84-6
Fleming, George A. 129
    Jane 128
    Josephus 128
    Martha A. 128
    W. H. 128-9, 156
Fletcher, J. B. 38
Flower, J. H. 38
Fookes, Alzada E. 77

Ford, Daniel 7
    Dillon 44
    J. Hardin 130
    James H. 134
    Marion 134
    Martha P. 130
    Ollie 134
    Thomas 37
Foust, W. M. 118
Frank, Ben T. 71
Free, John 12
Freeman, A. H. 70
    Albert Howard 74
    Catherine 74
    Henry 74
    L. L. 63
    Leon Lewis 68
    May V. 74
    T. M. 37
    W. A. 102
Frizzell, John 91
    Laura 86

–G–

Gaines, Sam 83
    Samuel 42
Gamble, H. C. 119
Gant, J. W. 53
Gardner, Dave 100
    Peter W. 37, 58
Gibson, G. 48, 137
    Granville 49
    William 7
Gilbert, Ambrose 45
    H. 48
    Hugh 38, 45, 49, 64
    Hugh Sr. 38
    J. C. 33, 36, 42, 64, 105, 122
    Jesse C. 33, 36
    Joel 4, 37
    John 38
Gingles, J. T. 100
Glenn, J. C. 34
    T. L. 33
Goheen, J. H. 117
    J. M. 53
    J. N. 92
    Laura 94
    T. L. 38
    T. L. Jr. 35, 36-7, 58, 130

Goheen, T. L. Sr. 35, 64
    Thomas L. Sr. 33
Goodall, Judith L. 95
Goodman, Elijah 7
    Thomas 7
Gossett, Alice 97
    Isaac 97
    L. J. 97
    Lizzie 97
    Susan 97
Grace, A. A. 109
    Jennie 109
    M. B. 109
Graham, J. W. 34
    Samuel 34, 71
Graves, Dr. 72
Gray, John 7
    Rayden 8
    S. 27
Grear, Johnathan 59
Green, C. M. 140
    D. M. 38, 55, 56, 57, 105
    E. G. 105
    George 50, 51
    James 50, 51
    Lillie G. 140
    Martha 55
    Martha E. 105
    Rachael 55
    S. T. 51
    T. J. 51
Greer, James 7
    Mrs. Joe 158
    W. D. 158
Gregory, Anna 100
    Elzada L. 75
    Laura 94
    Marion 94
    Oscar T. 94
Griffeth, B. B. 70
Griffith, Bird 60
    Jepthah 7
Grindall, Benjamin 8
Groves, S. C. 101
Grubbs, John T. 60
    T. T. 38
    Thomas A. 91
    Velina 60

-H-

Hall, B. T. 55, 56, 71, 73
    Benjamin T. 112-3
    Bethel 63
    Harrison 39
    John 112, 137
    Lena B. 112
    Linnie F. 112
    Lizzie 112
    Maggie L. 112
    Mintie L. 112
    Rebecca B. 112
    T. H. 157
Halton, Lane 52
Ham, J. H. 50
Hamilton, Claude H. 110, 127
    Eliza 127
    Elta 127
    Ethel 110
    John H. 91, 127
    McDonald 42
    Oddie 127
    Ruth 135
    Ruth J. 127
    Sarah M. 110, 127, 135
    W. B. 50, 110, 135, 157
    Mrs. W. B. 135, 160
    William B. 127
Hand, Henry 4, 34, 36, 38, 60, 64
Hanks, Elizabeth 55
Hanna, C. 109
Hanson, Lewis A. 40
Hardin, T. W. 51
Harold, Parker 11
Harp, Wiley 49
Harper, E. T. 122
    Elizebeth 103, 104
    William 104
Harris, Elihu 63, 111
    Ella 126
    J. L. 111
    Julius L. 125-6
    Sarah 111, 125
    T. M. 111, 125
Harrison, B. J. 136, 137
    Louisa J. 137
    Margaret W. 136
    S. T. 63

Harrison, T. F. 48, 49, 81, 102, 113, 136-7
    Thomas F. 38, 48, 77
Hartley, Flora 140
    Melissa 140
    W. A. 139-40
Hartsfield, T. I. 63
Hayden, R. 120
Haydock, J. G. 38, 96
    James G. 137
Haymes, J. L. 13
    Jarrett 57, 64
Heath, Ada A. 131
    Augusta 115
    Cora L. 131
    Elizabeth 82
    Emma 82
    Floy 63
    H. M. 36, 81-2, 87, 115, 119
    Jane 131
    Mertie E. 131
    P. J. 131
    R. B. 131-2
Hefley, W. G. 128
Helm, Governor 35
    J. M. 38, 73
    T. B. 70
    Thomas B. 73-4
Henderson, Lewis 43
    R. 77
Hendrick, J. J. 92
Henry, Colonel 40
    W. H. F. 130
Henson, Bartlet 8
    Calvin 12
    E. A. 70
    J. N. 63
    James 48
    L. V. 63
Hibbs, Lucy 33
Hickman, J. J. 58
Hiett, J. W. 133
    John 44
    Mary A. 133
Higgins, F. A. 63
Hill, J. R. 54, 55
    Jonathan 8
    Maggie 63
    Thomas 8
Hodge, Collin 105
Holland, Dr. 72
    Mr. 27

Holland, Basil 33
    H. B. 63
    Henry 94-5
    J. L. 67, 94
    J. N. 63
    J. W. 85
    James N. 67-8
    Jane 63
    John 49
    Lucas 63, 92
    M. A. 94
    Mary 64, 67
    W. A. 35, 36, 38, 41, 53, 58, 64, 83, 141, 148
    W. C. 33, 64, 94
    W. M. 92
Holmes, R. 52
Holsapple, J. W. 53, 54, 68
    John W. 53, 99
Holt, Dr. 72
Houser, J. M. 63
Houston, Attie 63, 106-7
    Ben 106, 107
    Boyd 107
    Crow 107
    Estella 107
    Flora 107
    Lena 107
    Maggie 107
    May 107
    Nellie 107
    Sam 107
    William 107
    Willie 107
Howard, Charles E. 70
    John 7
    Moffit 63
    Squire 9
    Stephen 7
Humphrey, R. E. 50, 51
Hunter, W. D. 34
Hurt, Lettis 13
    Rebecca F. 98
Hutchens, T. W. 48

-I-

Irvan, Dr. 72
    H. D. 97
    Hardin 56, 98
    John L. 33
    John T. 97, 98

Irvin, Dr. 116
Ivey, James H. 137, 138-9
    Martha Jane 138

-J-

Jackson, General 9
    A. T. 67
    Elizabeth 67
    G. W. 67
    Thomas 63
Jarrett, Nancy 64
Jenkins, J. P. 47, 48
    R. F. 141
    Samuel H. 33
Johnson, Augusta 115
    Elijah 42
    Huldah J. 115
    J. M. 38, 149
    J. W. 115
    James M. 115
    John 45
    Mamie 63
    Newton 49
    W. H. 115
Johnston, Absalom 8, 9
    Albert Sidney 10, 39
    Alfred 9-10, 33, 34, 35, 39, 80
    H. 37
    Isaac 8, 9
    J. H. 64
    J. O. 34, 38
    James H. 8-9
    William Henry 9
Jones, Mr. 8
    Charlie 63, 111-2
    E. J. 50
    Eliza 111
    G. S. 34, 37, 42, 81
    H. W. 63
    J. A. 71
    J. C. 118
    James R. 45, 54
    Jesse 7
    Lillie 104
    R. J. 111
    R. M. 70, 104
    S. S. 104
    Silas 104
    W. B. 38
    W. M. 38
Jordan, James 7

Joyce, Lillie 104
Justice, Dr. 72

-K-

Kahn, Oscar 85
Karnes, U. G. 63
Kelley, Dora 63
    J. E. 75
Kennedy, C. G. 46
    Charlie G. 47
    John 8
King, J. V. 46, 47
Kinkead, A. B. 95
Kirkpatrick, J. D. 46, 47
    M. J. 47
Knott, J. Proctor 83
Knox, Benjamin 7
    James 7

-L-

Lackey, Dr. 72
Lamb, Levi 7
Laremer, James 48
    Martha 48
    Penelope 48
Lawrence, Perry 7
Lawson, Mr. 8
Leckey, James 46
Lee, J. F. 53
    Joseph F. 53
    Levi 50, 95
    Sarah Jane 108
    W. P. 35
Leigh, William H. 50
Lemon, Clay G. 83
    Clay Galdstone 87
    Cora A. 83, 87
    J. R. 64, 87, 114, 118, 160
    James R. 82-4
    Lucretia C. 83
    Luna E. 83
    Maude S. 83
    Scott Thompson 83
Lemonds, Demarias A. 82
    J. G. 82
Lents, D. W. 63
    Davidson 133
    Elizebeth 133
    John T. 133-4, 143
    Mary A. 133

Lewman, M. 43
Lindsay, William 76
Lindsey, Caleb 56
    James 53, 54, 90, 95
    James Sr. 45
    Jesse 37
    Jesse A. 117
    John 56
    Polly 54
    Reuben 50
    William 54
Little, Beulah 118
    Francis 118
    Ida 118
    Isaac N. 118
    J. H. 37, 141
    Joseph H. 118-9
    Ruby May 118
    Thomas 118
Littlejohn, Charles 39
Locker, B. 50
    Freddie 61
    George W. 61
    Hellen M. 61
    Judith L. 95
    L. S. 91, 92
    Laban Shipps 95
Lockhead, John 91
Long, Hellen M. 61
    J. E. 92
    John E. 61
Love, E. G. 105
    James 91, 93
    Mrs. James 156
    Meta 93
    Thomas 91, 95
Lovett, D. A. 86, 118
    Elizabeth 86
    J. G. 67, 68, 94, 95
    John 86
    John G. 86-7, 158
    Lala 86
    Laura 86
Luter, Elisha 69
    Ida 63

-M-

McAtee, Charles W. 53
McBride, F. Norman J. 48
McCain, R. 76
    Robert 123
McClain, Lowery 55, 105

McClain, Sam 105
    William 105
McCoy, J. G. 90, 99
McCracken, Hugh 4
McCreary, James B. 79
McDonald, Mr. 7
McElrath, John T. 4
    Thomas 4, 43, 44
McElyea, Mrs. M. C. 53
McGee, J. M. 63
McGrigor, W. C. 49
    William 48, 49
McKinney, Mr. 8
    Bird 137
McKinnon, D. A. 44
    John 43
McLeod, J. C. 122
McManus, A. 48
McNabb, B. F. 42
Maddox, E. G. 63
Maldin, ——— 11
Mansfield, James 105
Marshall, C. C. 90
    Charles S. 42
    Edna E. 90
    John 3
Mathews, S. J. 112
    William B. 50, 51
Mathis, C. 42
    J. D. 63
    Samuel 64
Matthews, T. M. 53
Matthewson, Daniel 33
Maxwell, Captain 40
Mecoy, J. F. 45, 53
    John F. 54
Meloan, Sallie 78
Meyers, Joseph 53
Miller, Dr. 72
    C. E. 37
    George 58
    J. C. 38
    Willie P. 102
Minter, Henry L. 37, 42
    John 42
Mooney, J. M. 71
    Joseph M. 72
    Julia A. 72
    Mary A. 72
Moore, John 7
Morefield, J. W. 50
Morgan, James 7
    John 39

Morgan, John H. 40, 106
    R. O. 37
    Robert O. 4, 33
    Thomas 48
Morton, James 55
Murray, Jeremiah 8

-N-

Nall, J. J. 34
Nance, Daniel 8
    E. P. 52
    W. H. 52
Nanney, R. L. 63
Nelson, A. A. 37, 124, 138
    Amelia M. 124
    D. L. 53
Nimmo, W. W. 96
Norwood, John 53
    Melissa 140
Nuckolls, R. 72

-O-

Ogden, Parson 49
Ogilvie, John W. 33
Oliver, George W. 63, 109-10
    J. N. 109
    James N. 123
    Lucy V. 124
    Mary E. 109, 123
    Mike 144
    W. M. 109, 158
    W. Mike 123-4
Owen, Betsy 10
    Frances 10
    William 10
Owens, Ephram 105
    Williams 39
Owsley, William 79
Ozment, J. T. 37

-P-

Pace, Daniel 12-13, 38, 57, 64
    Elizabeth 82
    Hope 13, 64
    J. M. 53
    Langston 57
    Lettis 13
    M. B. 38, 63, 68
Palmer, Clemmie 89
    Ed 36

Palmer, Jake 41
    Lucy V. 124
    P. 42, 64, 79, 132
    Philander 4, 7, 34, 35, 36, 37, 41, 88, 136
    Solon L. 34, 50, 88-9, 130, 141, 142
    Susan A. 36, 88
    T. F. 34, 130
Park, D. G. 84
Park, Margaret 132
    Noah 132
Parker, Mr. 41
    C. 64
    M. B. 50
Parks, Joel 52
Parrish, G. W. 118
Paschal, Artely 99
Payne, Elder 47
Peay, Achilles 41
    William 41
Peck, L. O. 63
Pember, K. F. 139
Pendley, John W. 71
Penn, William 109
Penner, Dr. 72
Pennington, Alonzo 60
Perry, Hamilton 38
Peterson, J. D. 50, 141, 142, 155
    William N. 37
Phelps, M. V. 116
Philley, B. M. 63
    Calvin 45
Poiner, Mary A. 72
Pomroy, A. 64, 83
Pool, F. M. 42
Potts, Wesley 53
Powell, J. H. 75
Poyner, W. D. 48
Pryor, Judge 36
    Maggie L. 112
Puckett, Fannie 101
    S. C. 101
    W. 101
Pugh, Martha Jane 138
    J. T. 23, 26
Purcell, Samuel 40

-Q-

Quarles, J. M. 38

Quarles, R. P. 119
Quinn, J. M. 88

-R-

Randle, C. L. 88, 130
Ratcliffe, James 53
    Reason 39
Ray, Hicks 13, 51
    Hicks J. 139
    Mary P. 139
Reaves, Joseph 7
Reed, Boone 133
    Cecil 133
    Mrs. Henry 121
    Lula 133
    Margaret 132
    Mary Rosie 133
    N. R. 38
    Roscoe 133
    Rubie 133
    W. H. 121
    W. M. 33, 36, 66, 84, 110, 119, 123, 132-3, 158
    William 132
Reeder, Jesse 42
Reeves, David 126
    G. W. 33
    James 136
    Naomi 63
    Percilla J. 126
    William 39, 126
Rice, William 4
Riley, Mr. 18
    A. M. 88
    Ada 122
    G. W. 152
    George W. 121-2
    J. H. 34
    James H. 42
    Moses 34, 37, 38
    William 7
Risenhoover, N. E. 73
Roach, Briant 48
    N. B. 37
    Nancy 48
Robb, L. A. 63
Roberts, Mrs. Belle 69
    J. B. 50
    Martha E. 105
Robertson, Horace N. 71
    Horace Newton 116-7

Robertson, Lee 117
    T. M. 116
Rogers, D. F. 53
    Wiley 145
Rose, Robert 11
Rowland, M. C. 37, 55, 58
    R. E. 7
    Reuben 58, 59
Rucker, E. P. 102
Rudd, Bolivar 49
Rudolph, M. J. 47
Russell, Ella 126
    Ellie 101
    John G. 100
    T. S. W. 46
    Thomas E. 71
    Thomas Emmet 100-1
Ryan, Nat 154

—S—

Sargent, E. L. 63
Scott, Mr. 7, 8
Sears, B. F. 137
    Ben F. 38
Shelby, Isaac 12
Shelton, W. T. 64
Shemwell, David 42
    David A. 65
    Permelia J. 65
    Robert L. 34, 65-6
Shoat, Jane 131
Short, William 8
Shumaker, John 7
Sims, A. T. 53
    D. V. 63
    N. M. 66
Skaggs, Mr. 7
Slaughter, Elizebeth 133
    G. W. 133, 141
Sledd, Ed. S. 158
Smith, A. 50, 114
    Ab 92
    Absalom 4
    Alex 10
    D. G. 58
    Hastin 92
    J. R. 97, 141
    James 7
    Mrs. James P. 51
    Sarah M. 127, 135
Sneed, William 7
Speer, Lottie M. 73

Stamps, Tim 99
Starks, A. J. 38, 53
    C. H. 37, 38, 118,
        120-1, 125, 126
    Clara 114
    Edna 63
    Ella C. 121
    Emmet E. 121
    Helen B. 121
    Izora 114
    J. H. 40
    J. W. 149
    Jesse 57
    Jesse E. 121
    Julius 114
    L. C. 99, 139, 140
    Lillie G. 140
    Marshall 45, 52, 64
    Mary 98
    Mary A. 114, 120
    N. P. 99
    Nancy 64
    O. P. 99
    Oda 114
    R. H. 114, 150
    R. W. 97, 98-9, 140,
        141
    Rebecca F. 98
    Reuben 57
    Rufus H. 71
    Rupert M. 121
    S. H. 34, 38
    Spencer P. 98, 114, 120
    William M. 13, 53
    William Marshall 54, 57
    Winona 140
Staton, Charles 9
    Felix 39
    Jack 9
    Joseph 4, 9
    W. C. 56
Stephens, J. A. 151
    J. M. 35, 53
    John M. 53
Stewart, J. W. 98
    James 7
Stice, James 4, 35
Stilley, J. M. 58
    John M. 37, 114
    Katie E. 115
    Marshal 115
    Mary 115
    S. E. 114

Stilley, V. A. 114-5
    Van 50
    Van A. 70
Stone, E. W. 63, 66-7
    Ellen 66
    Hardin 64
    J. F. 73
    J. T. 38
    John P. 66
    John W. 73
    Lottie M. 73
    Lou. 18
    N. E. 73
    R. F. 34, 36, 38, 39
    W. J. 33
    W. S. 92
    William H. 38
    William S. 70
    William Speer 73
Story, James 37
Stratton, Mr. 8
Strow, Clara 114
    Clay W. 129
    D. Clinton 129
    Izora 114
    J. H. 64, 114
    John H. 64
    Katie E. 115
    Mary Rosie 133
    T. J. 115, 129, 151
    Willis 78
Styers, Emma 65
Sutherland, Reverand 50
    Rhoda 51

-T-

Tate, James W. 133
Tecumseh 12
Thomas, A. W. 38
    Cartha Belle 113
    E. G. 70
    E. J. 113
    Edmund G. 113
    J. H. 53
    J. S. 113
    Jesse 7
Thompson, A. P. 10
    D. D. 38
    Henry 7
    J. Q. 37
    Lucretia C. 83
    Martha 55, 83

Thompson, William 64
Trabe, Mr. 7
Tice, Mr. 42
    W. W. 42
Tilghman, Samuella 76
Tisdale, Mr. 7
Travis, T. A. 92
Treas, Mollie 63
Troutt, Mrs. I. B. 53
    J. R. 37
    Tennessee I. 53
Truitt, W. R. 120
Tubbs, Elzada L. 75
    J. P. 56, 57
    James P. 75
Tulley, J. C. 53
Turner, Oscar 33
Twitty, Mr. 7
Tyree, Fannie 101
    R. T. 52

-U-

Utley, Murrell 7
    W. A. 53

-V-

Vaughn, Jack 127
    John 51
Veech, Elijah 7

-W-

Wade, Banister 7
    H. M. 37
    Hardin M. 76
    Samuella 76
    William 10
Wake, R. W. 82, 84
Wallace, A. M. 88
    Eli 42
    Guy 88
    I. E. 56, 57, 88
    Ina 88
    L. E. 65
    Louis 63
    Louis E. 38, 88
    Louisa J. 137
    Sarah 88
Waller, Benjamin Rush 40
    T. B. 83
    Thomas B. 39

Waller, Wiley 13, 33, 40
Walters, W. B. 46
Ward, William 46
Warder, J. W. 55
Washam, Frances 10
    Ike 13
    Isaac 51, 139
    Lucy 11
    Mary P. 139
    Nelson 51
    Peter 10, 11
    Peyton 11
Washburn, Eliza 127
    Gabriel 127
Watkins, E. 48, 137
Watson, J. M. 90, 146
    Samuel 7
Wear, A. H. 145
    Annie B. 90
    Archibald H. 89
    Archibald Hugh 78
    Edna E. 90
    Estelle 90
    James V. 89-90
    Sallie 78, 89
    William O. 89
Weathers, W. L. 85
Weaver, J. B. 134
Webb, C. H. 33
Wells, A. J. 110
    Ethel 110
    J. K. 86
    M. A. 110
West, R. W. 63
Whale, N. A. 77
    Stephen A. 76-7
White, James D. 132
Whiteside, William 8
Whitnel, J. W. 64
Whittaker, Ben 107
Whittemore, Susan A. 36
Williams, Mr. 7
    Boaz 99
    Henry B. 37
    Hezekiah 7
    Morgan 45
    Nehemiah 7
    O. T. 38
    Robert 7, 105
    Stephen 7
Willoughby, A. T. 63
Wills, May V. 74
Wilson, Cora A. 83

Wilson, Mrs. Geraldine H. 55
    J. B. 71
    W. J. 37, 38, 58, 130, 160
Winfrey, Mr. 7
Wolf, Elder 47
Wood, Cartha Belle 113
    Josiah 64, 113
Woodall, J. M. 70
    Matilda 13
Woods, Mr. 8
    Jane 128
    Maude 119
    W. A. 119
Worrell, W. W. 137
Wortham, John 4
Wyatt, McGilberry 49
    Samantha A. 90

-Y-

Yeates, Joel 8

-Z-

Zueckler, E. 154
    Edward 92-3

****

www.ingramcontent.com/pod-product-compliance
Lightning Source LLC
Chambersburg PA
CBHW060356080526
44583CB00012B/345